Global Competitiveness

William Philip Wall

Global Competitiveness

Ten Things Thai Businesspeople Should Know

Strategies to improve competitive position and consolidate gains at rivals' expense

Springer

William Philip Wall
Faculty of Business and Technology
Stamford International University
Bangkok, Thailand

ISBN 978-981-16-7754-0   ISBN 978-981-16-7755-7 (eBook)
https://doi.org/10.1007/978-981-16-7755-7

© The Editor(s) (if applicable) and The Author(s), under exclusive license to Springer Nature Singapore Pte Ltd. 2022
This work is subject to copyright. All rights are solely and exclusively licensed by the Publisher, whether the whole or part of the material is concerned, specifically the rights of translation, reprinting, reuse of illustrations, recitation, broadcasting, reproduction on microfilms or in any other physical way, and transmission or information storage and retrieval, electronic adaptation, computer software, or by similar or dissimilar methodology now known or hereafter developed.
The use of general descriptive names, registered names, trademarks, service marks, etc. in this publication does not imply, even in the absence of a specific statement, that such names are exempt from the relevant protective laws and regulations and therefore free for general use.
The publisher, the authors and the editors are safe to assume that the advice and information in this book are believed to be true and accurate at the date of publication. Neither the publisher nor the authors or the editors give a warranty, expressed or implied, with respect to the material contained herein or for any errors or omissions that may have been made. The publisher remains neutral with regard to jurisdictional claims in published maps and institutional affiliations.

This Springer imprint is published by the registered company Springer Nature Singapore Pte Ltd.
The registered company address is: 152 Beach Road, #21-01/04 Gateway East, Singapore 189721, Singapore

In the business world, the rearview mirror is always clearer than the windshield.

—Warren Buffet

Introduction

How does a business distinguish itself from the competition? How does it develop competitiveness strategies? How can success be defined? What is the secret to success?

Competitive edge is sought by many countries today through higher growth rate and lower cost of production. These countries also realize that they must be innovative and invest to raise that competitiveness and productivity.

Through an open economy, Thailand derives approximately 60% of its GDP from exports. While cheap labor used to provide a competitive edge in Thailand, its surrounding neighbors and global economics have made that factor negligible. Because of the relatively low rate of investment and minimal increase in productivity, Thailand is in danger of being passed by in the global economic market.

Thailand is changing in many aspects. A military coup, which took power in September 2006, has been replaced by a rudimentary coalition of democratically elected officials. Investment in Thailand by foreign companies has slowed down due to the political uncertainty that surrounds the laws of investment and potential for growth and profit, while the baht has increased in strength by almost 25% against the US dollar over the past five years and challenged the profits of export industries.

The book is written as a guide and a manual for Thai business people who look to achieve and maintain a viable business environment in the global community. It is not meant as a criticism, but meant to develop a better awareness of doing business in the global economy and discuss some of the strategies Thai business people can use to develop a more competitive edge when doing business with global partners.

If you currently have a business and are successful, then you may not feel the need to read this book. Global competition, however, is not static and what works today may not work tomorrow. For as competitive as you are today, there is always someone looking over your shoulder to enter your market and take your customers. With the onset of the WTO and liberalization of trade, global competition is not a goal. Global competition is a never-ending journey that we must keep pace with or face potential failure.

The ideas and contents of this book are not meant to guarantee competitive success. They are meant to have you stop and think about what you are doing.

Contents

1	**Global Competition—The Battlefield**		1
	1.1	Scope of Business Competition	1
	1.2	Types of Competition	2
	1.3	Forms of Competition	2
		1.3.1 Perfect Competition	2
		1.3.2 Monopoly Competition	3
		1.3.3 Monopolistic Competition	4
		1.3.4 Oligopoly Competition	4
	1.4	Dynamic Competition in the New Era	5
2	**Marketing—Position Yourself**		7
	2.1	Definitions of Marketing	7
	2.2	Practicing Marketing	8
	2.3	Marketing and Thai Culture	9
	2.4	Applying the 4P's of Marketing	10
		2.4.1 Product	10
		2.4.2 Price	11
		2.4.3 Place	12
		2.4.4 Promotion	12
		2.4.5 Positioning Strategies	14
		2.4.6 Developing a Position Statement	15
		2.4.7 Identifying Current Market Position	15
		2.4.8 Analyzing Competitor Positioning	16
		2.4.9 Developing a Unique Position	16
3	**Innovate—Generate and Evaluate**		17
	3.1	Business Innovation	17
	3.2	Applying the Four Types of Innovation	18
		3.2.1 Incremental Innovation	18
		3.2.2 Disruptive Innovation	19
		3.2.3 Architectural Innovation	19
		3.2.4 Radical Innovation	19

		3.3	The Business Innovation Process	20
		3.3.1	Step 1: Idea Generation and Mobilization	20
		3.3.2	Step 2: Advocacy and Screening	21
		3.3.3	Step 3: Experimentation	21
		3.3.4	Step 4: Commercialization	22
		3.3.5	Step 5: Diffusion and Implementation	22
	3.4		Challenges to Innovation and Support Services in Thailand	23
4	**Using Information—Leverage Resource**			27
	4.1		Information as a Resource	27
	4.2		Existing Forms of Information	28
	4.3		Basic Sources of Information	29
	4.4		Leverage Business Information/Knowledge to Create Value	30
		4.4.1	Leveraging Business Information	30
		4.4.2	Information in Driving Revenue	30
		4.4.3	Improving Operational Efficiency	31
		4.4.4	Improving Customer Focus	32
		4.4.5	Gaining Competitive Advantage	32
		4.4.6	Setting Realistic Goals	33
5	**Technology—Upgrade**			35
	5.1		Technology in Business	35
	5.2		Steps to Follow When Upgrading Your Business Technology	36
		5.2.1	Step 1: Identify Technological Loopholes	36
		5.2.2	Step 2: Pilot Operation	37
		5.2.3	Step 3: Communication Plan	37
		5.2.4	Step 4: Training	38
		5.2.5	Step 5: Preparing Infrastructure	38
		5.2.6	Step 6: Implementation and Support	39
		5.2.7	Step 7: Performing Upgrade Review	39
	5.3		Benefits of Upgrading Technology in Business	39
		5.3.1	Increased Productivity	40
		5.3.2	Security of Data	40
		5.3.3	Attracting More Customers	41
		5.3.4	Cost Minimization	41
		5.3.5	Solving Problems	41
	5.4		Technology Transfer/Access to Technology	42
		5.4.1	Barriers to Technological Transfer	42
6	**Human Resources/Cross-cultural Communication—Breed Success**			45
	6.1		Human Resource Development	45
	6.2		Cross-cultural Communication Awareness	46
	6.3		Focusing HRM Communication Towards Business Missions	47
		6.3.1	Strategic Communication	48

		6.3.2	Communicating Human Resources Benefits and Risks	48
		6.3.3	Functional Implementation	48
	6.4		Creating Effective Communication Within the Organization	49
	6.5		Human Resource as a Business Asset	49
		6.5.1	Human Capital	50
		6.5.2	Possess Skills and Knowledge	50
		6.5.3	Contribution to Profits	50
	6.6		Creating Company Culture that Breeds Success	51
	6.7		Developing Cross-cultural Communication	51
	6.8		Developing of Cultural Intelligence	52
7	**Strategic Alliance—Strength in Numbers**			55
	7.1		The Spirit of Strategic Alliance	55
	7.2		Establishing a Strategic Alliance	56
	7.3		Advantages of Strategic Alliance	56
	7.4		Disadvantages of Strategic Alliance	57
	7.5		The Power of Partnerships	57
		7.5.1	Access to New Customers	58
		7.5.2	Building Brand Trust	58
		7.5.3	Developing New Perspectives	58
		7.5.4	Increased Moral Support	59
	7.6		Types of Strategic Alliances	59
		7.6.1	Pro-competitive Alliance	59
		7.6.2	Competitive Strategic Alliance	59
		7.6.3	Non-competitive Strategic Alliance	60
	7.7		Making It Work	60
		7.7.1	Picking a Partner	60
		7.7.2	Structuring the Agreement	61
		7.7.3	Managing the Deal	62
	7.8		Negotiation Styles and Strategies in Thailand	62
		7.8.1	Cultural Considerations During Negotiations	63
		7.8.2	Negotiation Styles	65
8	**Customer Service—Listen to What They Say**			67
	8.1		Active Listening to Customers	67
	8.2		How to Listen to Customers	68
	8.3		Importance of Listening to Customers	69
		8.3.1	Improved Relationship with the Customers	69
		8.3.2	Creating New Customers	69
		8.3.3	Avoiding Crisis	70
	8.4		Keeping the Conversation Going	70

9 Implementation, Monitoring and Evaluation—Now What Do We Do? ... 73
- 9.1 Now What Do We Do? ... 73
- 9.2 Implementation ... 74
  - 9.2.1 How to Carry Out a Successful Implementation ... 74
  - 9.2.2 Communication of the Strategic Business Plan ... 74
  - 9.2.3 Developing the Implementation Structure ... 75
  - 9.2.4 Developing Implementation Support Policies and Programs ... 75
  - 9.2.5 Budget and Resource Allocation ... 75
  - 9.2.6 Discharging Implementation Activities ... 76
  - 9.2.7 Avoiding Business Implementation Pitfalls ... 76
  - 9.2.8 Weak Strategy ... 76
  - 9.2.9 Ineffective Staff Training ... 77
  - 9.2.10 Poor Communication ... 77
  - 9.2.11 Poor Follow Through ... 77
- 9.3 Monitoring and Evaluation ... 78
  - 9.3.1 Developing Monitoring and Evaluation Strategy ... 78
  - 9.3.2 Defining Measurable Benchmarks ... 78
  - 9.3.3 Communicating Benchmarks ... 78
  - 9.3.4 Developing Monitoring Plans ... 79
  - 9.3.5 Establishment of the Review Plans ... 79
- 9.4 Benefits of Monitoring and Evaluation in Business Strategies ... 79
- 9.5 Challenges of Monitoring and Evaluation Process ... 80

10 Social Responsibility—Giving Something Back ... 81
- 10.1 Giving Something Back ... 81
- 10.2 Giving Back to Business ... 82
- 10.3 Ways to Give Back to Society ... 82
  - 10.3.1 Getting Your Employees Involved ... 83
  - 10.3.2 Setting Aside Part of the Profits ... 83
  - 10.3.3 Being Part of the Community ... 84
  - 10.3.4 Building Communities ... 84
- 10.4 Moral Obligation and Corruption ... 84
- 10.5 Benefits of Giving Back to the Society ... 85
  - 10.5.1 Improved Business Reputation ... 85
  - 10.5.2 Attracting Talent ... 86
  - 10.5.3 Building Connections and Widening Business Networks ... 86
- 10.6 The Cost of Ignoring Social Responsibility ... 86
- 10.7 Using Social Responsibility to Build a Sustainable Business ... 87
  - 10.7.1 Building Your Social Responsibility Strategy Around Your Core Competencies ... 87

	10.7.2 Recognizing the Important Social Issues to Your Customers	88
	10.7.3 Motivating Your Employees	88
10.8	Bottom Line	88

References 91

Chapter 1
Global Competition—The Battlefield

Abstract This chapter discusses businesses competition and the need for firms to understand their competition, the competitive nature of business and the need to set your firm apart from in order to survive tough business terrain. Types and forms of competition are discussed to show different manifestations of competition and the dynamic nature of competition with the emergence of new technologies.

1.1 Scope of Business Competition

In many business environments, companies compete against each other for customers, by offering cheaper or better-quality products and services, as compared to their competitors. The survival of a company depends on its ability to successfully compete with its rivals. As a result, the question that arises is, "what is competition?" Inferring from Tallman et al. (2018), competition refers to the rivalry in the marketplace, by companies, which sells similar products or services, with an objective of achieving higher revenue, profit and market share. The major thing about competition is that is always exists in the business environment. However, some environments are fiercely competitive while others are less competitive.

To compete effectively in the market, a business needs to be aware of what its competitor(s) is doing. This implies the range of products and/or services offered by the competitor, their prices, quality, and other strategies adopted in their business operations. With that, the concerned business can compete by offering more value to the customers as compared to the competitors. The additional value offered to the competitor may be in form of cheaper price, after sales service, superior products and/or services among other metrics.

In addition to being aware of the competitors, it is equally critical to be aware of the tastes, preferences, needs and wants of the targeted customers, as well as the changes in these aspects (Harrison et al., 2000). Conducting market research and development and ability to offer unique, differentiated, and new products could give a business in a competitive advantage. Once consumers purchase a product or service and are satisfied with it, they will typically purchase the same product again. Having a competitive advantage means that a company does something better than its competitors (Luo, 2007). Competitive advantage could be gained from adopting and implementing various aspects such as developing and introducing a new and needed product in the market, offering similar products at a cheaper price, offering high quality products and/or services at the same price, better customer services, or applying advanced technology.

1.2 Types of Competition

When we talk of competition in the business market, the next question that rings in mind is what type of competition. There are three types of competition, or three types of competitors:

Direct Competition—direct competition, as the name implies, is when competitors are in the same line of business, and are offering similar products and/or services as you are (Crowley & Jordan, 2017). These competitors are referred to as direct competitors. When business competition is mentioned, the first thing that comes to mind is the direct competition. However, competition revolves around anything targeted by the competitor, such as price, service, sales point, particular product or service attribute, etc.

Indirect Competition—Indirect competition refers to situations where competitors offer the same product or service, but through different markets or business goals and have adopted different business strategies in their business operations. These competitors are referred to as indirect competitors. Their market strategies are also different.

Replacement Competition—In this type of competition, the competitors offer different products and services as compared to you, but the customer can opt to purchase them instead of your products or service. In other words, 'the customer can replace your purchase for their purchase'. This means that you and the competitors are competing for resources. It is the most difficult type of competition to identify in the market.

1.3 Forms of Competition

1.3.1 Perfect Competition

Perfect competition refers to a situation characterized by many competitors offering similar products and services. Due to the high number of competitors selling similar products, there are many substitutes available to consumers. In this form of competition, there is no seller with any significant influence on the market, and thus prices are determined by the forces of demand and supply. According to Azevedo and Gottlieb

(2017), in a perfect competition market situation, it can be assumed that the concept of consumer preference does not exist, since the buyers have perfect information regarding the past, present, and future products sold in the market and the prices charged by each seller.

It can be articulated that perfect competition results in various benefits. For instance, there are no barriers to entry into the perfectly competitive market, thus sellers cannot create monopoly power. Similarly, the buyers in this form of competition have perfect knowledge about the products and firms selling the products, there is thus, no need to spend on advertising (Azevedo et al., 2017). Also, due to the lack of barriers to entry, firms only make normal profits and the producers only cover their opportunity costs.

However, also, the perfect competition market comes with bottlenecks. For example, operating under a perfectly competitive market does not allow for the utilization of economies of scale by the sellers. The existence of the no barrier to entry allows a high number of firms to operate under this form of market competition leading to targeting of normal profits only (Azevedo et al., 2017). Similarly, in this form of competition, the markets lack the use of innovation and technology. The ability for sellers to share information leads to a lack of incentive to develop new technologies and investment in Research and Development (R&D) which leads to improved market operations.

1.3.2 Monopoly Competition

In a monopoly form of competition, the market is characterized by a single seller with monopoly power. In this competitive situation, the single firm with monopoly power controls the entire market and is responsible for setting prices it wishes. Under this form of competition also, the buyers do not have control of the prices as there are limited alternatives (Xing Li, 2015). The consumers are thus the price takers. The forces of demand and supply are not relevant in this competitive market, making it extremely undesirable. Similarly, there are barriers to entry enabling the firm with monopoly power to maintain super-normal profits.

Firms operating in a monopoly form of competition accrue various benefits. Firms with monopoly power benefit from the economics of scale, due to single firms controlling the resources. According to Parenti (2017), monopoly power is vital in generating dynamic efficiency including technological advancements. Business innovation can be achieved by large firms enjoying monopoly power compared to firms in competitive markets. Benefiting from the economies of scale helps the firms to make high profits that can be invested in research and development projects (R&D). Single firms with monopoly power can dominate domestic markets, making it easier for them to penetrate other markets abroad.

Monopoly competition can, however, be criticized due to its negative impacts on the consumers. The restrictive entry to the monopoly market spells negative effects on the consumers who have no control over the prices of products in the market (Hawley,

2015). Operating under the monopoly market also limits consumer choice, since all products are produced by a single firm. Similarly, this form of competition restricts the output into the market, compared to the situation under a perfect competition market.

1.3.3 Monopolistic Competition

The monopolistic competition is considered the most market realistic scenario. The monopolistic competition structure combines the characteristics of the oligopoly and perfect competition structures. Under the monopolistic competition structure, there is free entry and exit in the market by sellers, with differentiation of products (Bertoletti & Etro, 2017). However, in the long run, the supernormal profits attract more sellers into the market–leading to normal profits. The lack of barriers to entry attracts many firms to the market–leading to allocative and productivity inefficiency from the sellers.

Operating under a monopolistic competition benefits sellers, examples of businesses operating under the monopolistic competition model include restaurant businesses, consumer services including hairdressing, and hotels among other businesses. Under monopolistic competition, therefore, the firms benefit from the limited barriers to entry. Monopolistic markets are thus contestable by all interested businesses. Dhingra and Morrow (2019), also argue that under the monopolistic model, the firms are dynamically efficient in terms of innovation and development of new products to gain a competitive edge over rivals.

The monopolistic competition model is, however, limited in various ways. Competition under monopolistic competition forces firms to perfect in differentiation to achieve supernormal profits. Thus, firms better in brand differentiation are likely to operate in a form of oligopoly competition and will be able to make supernormal profits (Zeuthen, 2018). Similarly, brand differentiation in the monopolistic competition can lead to strong brand loyalty, which may turn out to be a barrier to entry to other firms to the market.

1.3.4 Oligopoly Competition

Oligopoly competition refers to a market structure where a small number of firms have a significant influence on the market. Some of the business types operating under the oligopolistic competition model include the fuel retailing businesses, the banking businesses, cinema, among other businesses. Competition under the oligopolistic structure is characterized by interdependence. Since only a few firms are operating under this competition, one firm's decisions need to take into account the reaction of the close rivals (Taylor, 2014). For instance, a single firm's decision to lower prices may lead to retaliatory action from rivals who may lower their prices further to maintain their competitive edge. Similarly, the oligopolistic competition market has natural entry barriers due to economies of large-scale production, control of key scarce resources by few firms, and often predatory pricing.

In businesses, cooperation is often highly rewarding, and firms operating under an oligopolistic competition model stand to gain in various ways. In most cases, firms adopt a competitive strategy similar to those in more competitive markets to their benefit (Yan, 2017). For example, firms under oligopolistic competition may agree to compete in other areas excluding price. In addition, operating under this competitive market leads to dynamic efficiency, since firms can invest in research and development from the extra profits earned.

However, also, the oligopolist competition has various disadvantages to the firms under this model. In some instances, the barriers to entry under oligopoly can be deliberate. Often the few firms operating under a monopoly may opt to bar rivals at all costs to their advantage including the use of government regulations with oligopoly-based interests (Head, 2017). Other deliberate barriers to entry into the oligopolistic competition market include operating on the economies of scale allowing for lower prices and the high start-up costs involved.

1.4 Dynamic Competition in the New Era

Competition is inescapable during the life form of any business operation and expansion. With technological advancements in the society, the nature of competition has changed. Further developments of internet technology and the introduction of big data to business has brought in a form of dynamism where data that was relevant yesterday will become obsolete today with new information about the target user demographic (Pi et al., 2017). The dynamic nature of the competition means that has brought in a situation where firms do not know who their competition will be in the future, new business models come up every day that challenge the traditional forms of businesses as we know them. The big movie studios in Hollywood never anticipated that a movie rental platform like Netflix would become the biggest rival to studios (Feldman, 2019; Hadida et al., 2021). The challenge has seen many studios set up similar online platforms and release movies on the internet first before studios or release both online and for studios to minimize the impact of the competition (Netflix).

Big data has ushered in an era of rich and comprehensive user information that are extracted from users' purchase history, search history, and browsing history. This has made competition among rival firms more sophisticated and dangerously personalized to a point that raises privacy concerns among marketing watchdogs and regulators. In response to the dynamic nature of competition today, businesses should optimally manage dynamic competition with competitors by understanding the minutiae of the market segment, scaling up or downsizing to meet the needs of your customers, and ensure resources are optimally utilized for the operation, viability, and long-term sustenance of the business venture.

Similar competition variables are applicable when considering taxi drivers and cab haling companies online. Taxi drivers saw each other as the competition and would devise means such as keeping the taxi clean, using sweet smelling perfumes, or playing music to suit their customers to attract passengers. However, the introduction of online hailing companies like Uber and Lyft introduced a dynamism where the competition were no longer fellow taxi drivers, but new companies that had better looking cars, and catered to business executives and Millennials (Cramer & Krueger, 2016; YvKoff, 2020). Thus, for businesses to survive, it is essential to understand the business and user demographic, and meet their needs accordingly.

Chapter 2
Marketing—Position Yourself

Abstract This chapter discusses marketing as a concept of positioning the firm or its product to beat out competition. Different definitions of marketing are put forward as well as practicing marketing. Marketing is also discussed with respect to Thai culture and the need to understand the market segment that marketing campaigns intend to target. The 4p's of the marketing mix are highlighted, and the chapter ends with how brands can position themselves in the business market.

2.1 Definitions of Marketing

In the current competitive business environment, marketing has established itself as an indispensable tool. As a business entity, there are always various questions that need to be addressed: What does the customer want? Do my customers trust my products? Do customers prefer my products and/or services as compared to those of my competitors? What are the complaints and compliments of customers regarding my products and/or services? The answer to all the questions, among other similar questions lies in the concept of marketing (Olson et al., 2018; Sawmong, 2020a). So, the question that comes to mind is, 'what is marketing?' Various definition exists, which have made effort to explain what marketing really is. The Oxford Dictionary defines marketing as:

> the action or business of promoting and selling products or services, including marketing research and advertising

The American Marketing Association defines marketing as:

> the activity, set of instructions, and processes for creating, communicating, delivering and exchanging offerings that have value for customers, clients, partners, and society at large.

On the other hand, Business Dictionary defines marketing as:

> "the management process through which goods and services move from concept to the customer." This definition is also extended to incorporate the 4P's of marketing, which include Product, Price, Place, and Promotion.

There are other researchers that have made effort in expounding the concept of marketing, such as Adel et al. (2020), who considered marketing as a systematic process involving the activities of planning, implementing and controlling a mixture of business activities, with an objective of facilitating meeting of buyers and sellers, for effective and mutually beneficial exchange of goods, services. In other words, marketing could be considered as the process determining the needs, wants, and preferences of the customers, to provide them with the goods and services, which meet, or even exceed their expectations.

Inferring from a professor of Business Administration at the Harvard Business School named Theodore Levitt, it is critical for business enterprises to incorporate effective marketing strategies in the business operations, to achieve a balanced orientation. He based his recommendations both on the academic research as well as the examination of companies that have adopted good and bad marketing strategies, and their outcomes. In his book, *The Marketing Imagination* Levitt states that:

> The search for meaningful distinction is a central part of the marketing effort. If marketing is seminally about anything, it is about achieving customer-getting distinction by differentiating what you do and how you operate. All else is derivative of that and only that. Differentiation represents an imaginative response to the existence of potential customers in such a way as to give them compelling reasons to want to do business with the originating supplier. To differentiate an offering effectively requires knowing what drives and attracts customers. It requires knowing how customers differ from one another and how those differences can be clustered into commercially meaningful segments. The discovery of the simple essence of things is the essence of the marketing imagination.
>
> Marketing is inescapable in the determination of corporate results. The reason is that marketing deals with the sources and levels of the revenues that help determine the corporate fate. Since marketing means getting and keeping customers in some acceptable proportion relative to competitors, it is to the marketing imagination one must look to gain differential advantage over competitors. In business, the marketing imagination is the central tool for deciding on what the purposes are to be. (Levitt 1983)

2.2 Practicing Marketing

Marketing involves not looking at your business as an insider. You need to ask how outsiders—your customers and suppliers—would look at your company. What would someone conclude and recommend after carefully looking at your business with new, unbiased eyes? Marketing can help your company create value for your product in a number of ways. Proper advertising and brand position can give your product a higher perceived value. The higher the perception of value the higher your company can price the product.

Consumer needs can be discovered and passed on to research and development teams, who can in turn create products with a greater perceived value and to match those needs. Research budgets can also be better allocated based on assessment of the potential market size of a particular product or customer need. However, while modern transportation and communication have helped to consolidate tastes and preferences among consumers, you must always be aware of the economic and cultural differences that continue to stop the standardization of even the largest brands in the global marketplace. A clear example of this is McDonald's selling a hot ham and cheese sandwich called the Croque, McDo in France and a chicken sandwich on Arabian bread under the name of McArabia.

So your marketing strategy must incorporate how your products are perceived, promoted, and used in relation to the country in which they are to be sold and utilized. Local tastes and preferences differ from country to country. In addition, product and technical standards and trade barriers may also prevent your company from selling a standardized product to a global marketplace using a standardized marketing strategy. It is naive to think that national marketers can dominate a global marketplace with national products.

So what is the basic goal of marketing? It is to find a need and fill that need. Marketing is a four-part function: product, price, place and promotion. The concept and eventual end result is to design a product the consumer wants, price it to be competitive, put the product somewhere that the consumer can easily find it and promote it so the consumer knows it exists. Constant research is critical. It determines opportunities and problems and presents information to make good decisions.

2.3 Marketing and Thai Culture

Thailand has been regarded as the home of "smiles" because of the disposition of the people to smile not considering the circumstance. Beyond the hospitable smiles driven in large parts by the growth of the hospitality business which has seen Bangkok as a top tourist destination ahead of global cities like London and Paris. In divergence with western culture where a smile denotes expressions of happiness, smile in Thai culture conveys different meanings; it could be feelings of happiness, confusion, anger, embarrassment or awkwardness. It is important to note that the smile regardless of the context reflects the self-control of the Thai, and the expression is their way of trying to assert control of the situation. This is called the "Mai Pen Rai" (It doesn't matter) mentality of the average Thai. The cultural justification linked to these smiles provides insights into consumer behavior in the Thai market that businesses need to understand and utilize to succeed (Hayes, 2011; More than Just Smiles, 2018).

Thailand is a modern country deeply steeped in tradition, and with a growing middle-income class who are traditionally considered as the backbone of any market as they are made up of groups that are willing to spend income compared to the traditionally wealthy who already have their market outlined from generations or the poor who do not have enough to spend. Analysis have shown that Thailand's middle-income class have a propensity to spend compared to other South East Asian economies, and this is evident in the higher debt profile of Thailand compared to its neighbors. This high spending habits of the Thai has been credited to their style of living in the moment and downplaying the impact of the present on the future. The Thais have a belief system that is largely shaped by Buddhism where emphasis is on the present, and what has happened previously is considered as the past and should stay in the past. Understanding concepts like this when introducing products in the

Thai market is essential because it runs contrary to western beliefs where emphasis is placed on the past because it shapes the future.

Firms can put themselves in healthy business situations by underlining the relevance of living in the moment, and providing goods and services that capture the essence of "the now" instead "later". The accentuation of pleasurable living in the moment with products and services would particularly be well-suited for categories of light indulgences. No wonder tourism industry is highly rated in Thailand where the priority is hedonistic and pleasurable experiences. This notion is seen to be applicable not just to tourism, but to other industries as well. Even though living in the moments entails more spending than saving, the banking industry specifically The Asian Development bank (ADB) delivered a "saving is cool" campaign targeted at people who got their first jobs through a portrayal of being a lifestyle guru, and characterizing "saving" as something ideal and noble.

In continuation of the living in the moment mentality, Thais consider "health" as the most basic measure of satisfaction and happiness in life. This is why a Thai will always pray for good health, wealth and fortune. They believe there is a relationship between good health and financial issues which would then hamper their enjoyment in the present. The need for good health among young Thais is even greater because health is associated with appearance, and the greater majority of Thais shun regular exercise. This they try to circumvent by patronage of healthier food vendors, supplements and gym related business. Plastic surgery has also gained popularity in Thailand because it is considered easier to look good by undergoing cosmetic surgery instead of eating and exercising regularly to maintain body shape and physique.

The high shopping habit of Thais has resulted in the emergence of convenience stores almost on every corner. The biggest convenient store chain has over 10,000 stores that service over 30 million shoppers on a weekly basis in Thailand. The convenience stores themselves have profited largely from increasing urbanization and chaotic traffic congestions which encourages Thais to shop at the nearest location to avoid worsening traffic situations. The ubiquity of the internet has also helped to increase the spending habit of over 44 million Thais who use mobile internet users (More than Just Smiles, 2018). Understanding these variables can be invaluable to prospective businesses and planning accordingly how to communicate and always understand the market is important to the operation and expansion of any business entity.

2.4 Applying the 4P's of Marketing

2.4.1 Product

Product refers to the goods and services that you are selling or rather offering to the market, as well as the experience of the targeted customer with your products or services. This P(product) involves finding good answers to various questions related

2.4 Applying the 4P's of Marketing

to the products or services you offer to the market, such as 'what makes the customers prefer your product or service rather than the competitors?' 'What problem does your product or service solve in the market?' 'Why are the goods and/or services you offer to the market considered attractive? Findings answers to those questions involves conducting an extensive evaluation of the underlying elements of the product or service offering to the market. For instance, a customer could be attracted to your products by its name, packaging, scent, ease of use, design, quality features or even the support services (Ackerman & Schibrowsky, 2007). It is critical to consider that through such factors the customer may interested in a particular product, the purchase itself would be influenced by particular factors such as buying experience.

Slater and Olson (2001) in their publication advices that it is vital for businesses to offer a product or service that solve a particular problem in the market and create memories with sentimental values. A product like the Thai silk will hold some value for a tourist to Thailand, it will be one of the reminders of fond memories they experienced in Thailand. The silk material can be made into products like scarfs, cushion or clothing. They are usually adorned in tropical bright colors that lead owners of such products to reminisce about the origin. Tourists looking to experience the full Thai experience can also consider products like local Thai clothes. Thai clothes are usually embroidered with vivid dazzling colors and animal or geometric subjects, in an easy stylish and universal design. One of the most popular designs with tourists to Thailand are pants embroidered with elephants pants or possibly a sundress because it's spacious, natural and a fit for the casual holiday outlay.

2.4.2 Price

Price is as simple as it sounds. However, the mechanism of pricing is important in determining whether customers will purchase your product or not. You may be offering a good product or service, having necessary features, but if it is wrongly priced, it may be difficult to make sales. Therefore, a businessperson should not price his products or services too high or too low, because people are more likely to purchase a product and/or service that is priced well. There are several factors that determine the pricing of a product. The most relevant factor is its quality. Customers should have a feeling that they get more value from the product and/or service than they are paying for. Other factors that significantly influence the price include the cost of goods or the cost of production, the distribution costs, other overhead costs that have direct influence on the price of a product. To have an effective price set for a product and/or service, then you have to establish a mechanism to balance the perceived value of the product, and the price set for selling the product. A product we can consider in the Thai context is the Thai coconut oil. There are numerous benefits to utilizing Thai coconut oil; it has been extensively applied in cosmetics and cosmetology, cooking and spa treatments. It is paramount to choose a product based on personal recommendations or preferences because a higher product price does not always translate into a higher quality product. While price may be indicative of a better quality product, this may not always be the case as with Thai coconut oil, it serves the customer better to buy products based on personal preference or function of the product to the customer. This ensures that customers get value for money instead of buying an expensive item that has no value to the buyer other than the feeling of just having an expensive item.

2.4.3 Place

Place refers to the "placement" or distribution of products. the marketing concept of place answers the questions on how the customers will be able to find and purchase the company's products and services. Product placement is vital in understanding how to market company products. For instance, if a company sells its products overseas or regionally, then doing local marketing would not make sense. In contrast, for local businesses, adopting a local advertising strategy will effectively save you costs. Thus, the idea of "Placement" helps you assess the most suitable channel for a product (Ikechi et al., 2017). Similarly, how the product is likely to be accessed by the customer is important in the product placement strategy. The common distribution channels under product placement include direct sales and wholesalers. However, with the increase in the development of online stores, shaping the overall customer experience is vital (Muangmee et al., 2021).

Analyzing the place of the restaurant business in Thailand is crucial to its survival. The global position of Thailand as a top tourist destination means the tourists will also need food while they are in the country. Thailand has a number of exquisite foods which also serve as part of the draw that attracts tourists. One way Thai food vendors have kept their clientele over the years is by selling on the street instead of decent enclosures. What this means is that there is direct contact between tourists and the food; both the aromatic scent and the sight of other people eating in the full glare of the street encourages tourists to join the food party. Most of the tourists in their own home countries may not consider street food, but because of the distance and the low chances of running into an acquaintance, it becomes easier for tourists to get into the Thai spirit and enjoy the various delicacies on offer. The strategy of selling food in the open street is one that has worked and will continue working for Thai food business owners who have thrived without fancy venues, some eat the whole thing standing and moving from stall to stall tasting different Thai cuisines as part of the tourist experiences.

2.4.4 Promotion

Promotion in marketing involves all the marketing strategies and techniques used to sell products. Businesses use different ways to communicate their products to their customers including advertising, public relations, and sales promotions among other

2.4 Applying the 4P's of Marketing

strategies. Inferring to Lahtinen et al. (2020) in the current marketing environment, marketers have a broad range of advertising including online marketing with a wide range of reach. While determining the suitable promotion strategy for products, you should consider the cost and the targeted end-users. You should therefore ask yourself questions such as; does it solve the needs of the customer? Is the message clear and tailored to the target audience? Some of the recent common promotional channels you can use may include TV adverts, social media marketing, podcasts, pay-per-click (PPC) ads among other channels. It is vital to understand that promotion differs from other marketing concepts as it involves only the aspect of communication to the customers. We shall consider the promotion strategies of Thai Airways, the flagship airline of Thailand and how their marketing strategies have positioned the brand in the competitive airline business which has been impacted globally by the COVID-19 pandemic.

The airline services a number of destinations in the world. Thai Airways has among its fleet aircrafts such as Airbus Boeing 777-200ER, Airbus A350-900, A330-300, Boeing 747-400, Boeing 777-200, Airbus A380-800, Boeing 777-300, Boeing 787-9, 777-300ER, and Boeing 787-8. Plans are underway to add newly-developed aircrafts to replace older models of Boeing 777 aircrafts. Some of the packages offered on Thai Airways include Royal First Class (First Class), Royal Silk Class (Business Class) and Economy Class as a part of its promotional efforts to market the airline globally. In efforts to market the airline to meet with the times, digital marketing is actively employed to reach its international customers and supported by ads in print and television. The airline has been known to also support its customers during festive periods by increasing the number of flights during such seasons to meet travel demands, and serving special desserts as part of introducing passengers to Thai cuisines. The company in addition runs a promotional campaign where visitors can select from five events such as Traditional Thai Dancing, Making Thai-styled floral garland, Muay Thai, Thai cooking and speaking Thai and submit to win a prize. Non-Thai participants have the opportunity to win a month free stay or a short stay holiday or a premium luxury adventure. Such campaigns have the potential to increase a brands likeness visibility on social media and also create awareness and favorability for the brand.2.5 Positioning Yourself in the Business Market.

Positioning in the business market involves influencing the customer perception regarding your product relative to the competitors. The objective of market positioning is to develop an identity of the products through which the consumers perceive them in a particular way. For instance, McDonald's has positioned itself as a place for quick and cheap meals, while Apple has established itself as a tech business with user-friendly products. The positioning of a business in the market thus involves various strategies including product attributes and benefits, prices of the products, quality, product use, and application, and the competition levels (Iyer et al., 2019). Therefore, creating an effective business market positioning requires a positioning strategy.

2.4.5 Positioning Strategies

Businesses aiming to take a strategic position in the markets need to identify how they want their products or services to be perceived by the consumers. There is thus a need to create and establish a particular product image or identity in the minds of the consumers in the target markets. As a seller, a good positioning strategy helps you to create the successful longevity of the business (Iyer, 2019). Active positioning also requires that the business positions itself with the right message, values, and experience to its customers. Positioning does not cover only the strengths of the company and products, but also those of its competitors and making sure your message resonates with these realities is essential. Positioning should not be focused on the product, but on the mind of the prospective customer and where they belong when associating with the brand (Ries & Trout, 1981). This is what the brand should strive for; every successful brand has a Unique Selling Preposition (USP). This refers to features and characteristics of brands and products that differentiate it from others with similar products. In the smartphones niche, Apple effectively differentiates its products from others, you will never find an Apply operating system (OS) IOS on other smartphones, but you can find the Android OS on many phone brands. Effectively, if you love the IOS operating system, you can only get it from an Apple phone. Apple has uniquely positioned itself in a way that sets it apart from the others. Similarly, the McDonald's franchise competes globally with thousands of fast food brands, what they consider as their USP is the family-themed nature of their business. They do not present themselves as the tastiest, fastest, or most affordable brand, but rather on the orientation that McDonald's is a place you can eat in a kid's friendly environment, children menu and toys, things that will make your children love outdoor.

There are various strategies you can use to position yourself in the business market, some of these include positioning based on product features, like electric vehicles will be positioned as eco-friendly, Toyota will talk about their reliability on the road, Volvo position their brand based on safety, Porsche does the same but allied to performance. Positioning based on price where the key word is "affordable," something considered a must-have in every home, or for every student, or for an age-range, it is usually mass targeted or to exploit a gap in the market by fixing your price to cover an existing gap. Positioning can also be based on quality or luxury. Here the target is exclusivity, and price is not a determinant here. In fact, the idea is to exclude certain category of people and the users see themselves as an elite and exclusive set. The preposition is to achieve success and reach this exclusive level or by keeping up appearances by remaining in this exclusive and elite group. Mercedes and Ferrari in the car manufacturing view themselves as elite and luxurious brands. It's important to note that positioning by luxury or quality does not often equate to superiority, what is does is give the users the perception of being superior and above others not using similarly pricey products.

2.4 Applying the 4P's of Marketing

2.4.6 Developing a Position Statement

A positioning statement refers to the identity that the business hopes to create in the market. While striving to position yourself in the business market, it is vital to understand the identity that your business is striving to create. The position statement, therefore, will be the basis of the business identity, from which point you can create a path in the business market. According to Jalkala and Keränen (2014), the development of an effective position statement would require identification of various market aspects and modeling them to the benefit of the business. For instance, you need to define the target audience, which will involve the identification of the characteristics of the consumers that the products will be targeted. By determining the target consumer tastes, preferences, and needs, the business will be able to position itself to cater to the needs and interests of these consumers.

The other aspects to consider in the development of an effective positioning statement includes, defining the target market, and creating a value position statement. For example, with the increase in online retailing, an online retail business should consider the consumer needs for fast and convenient delivery of products. The positioning statement therefore could be the key to business' marketing and advertising decisions (Lahtinen et al., 2020). Position statements should answer business-marketing questions such as; does it focus on the target audience and needs? And does the position statement offer real value? An effective position statement will positively impact the consumer's perception of your product thus positioning yourself well in the business market.

2.4.7 Identifying Current Market Position

Understanding your current market position is the starting point in developing your desired position in the market. The identification of the current market position helps in determining the new positioning path for the business that will set you apart from your competitors (Sarmaniotis et al., 2014). The identification of the business' current position will require answering the questions such as; what business the company currently does? And how good the company is doing in that business? The assessment will involve evaluation of the internal and external environments compared to that of the competition in the market. Internal evaluation of the business will involve primary resources that form the foundation of the business's performance such as, the business' financial resources, technological resources, human resources, and operating resources. Analysis of the internal aspects relating to the business's operations and success is essential in determining the strengths and weaknesses in relation to the competition and consequently identifying your position in the market. Effective assessment of the business helps you understand where you stand in relation to the competition and forms the basis for proper competing for your market share.

2.4.8 Analyzing Competitor Positioning

Understanding the competition in the business market helps determine the gaps that your business can fill. Thus, analyzing competition is critical in not only determining the strengths and weaknesses of the businesses, but also carving a position in the business market. While analyzing competition in the market, you need to take into account various aspects such as the competition's market history. As articulated by (Cristea, 2014), sellers striving to position themselves in the market, need to understand various historical aspects of the competition including the products and services they offer and how they market them to the customers, their distribution channels, and prices among other aspects. A clear understanding of the competition in the market will help you channel a business path that will make you stand out and well positioned. There are various ways you can learn about the competition in the market. These include analyzing their annual reports, carrying out online research on the businesses, and attending their exhibitions. While evaluating the information regarding market competition, you should be able to identify market gaps in the market that can be exploited, as well as determining the level of saturation of suppliers in particular areas in the market (Jalkala and Keränen, 2014). Creating an effective market position requires focusing on less competitive areas and striving to stand out from the competition.

2.4.9 Developing a Unique Position

Effective positioning in the business market requires the development of a unique position of your business in the market. After understanding the competition levels, the target market, and identifying the current position in the market, you should strive to create a unique position that sets you apart from the competition and other players in the market to ensure success (Sarmaniotis et al., 2014). The data on the business assessment helps you understand who you are and how you will model yourself to be the best in your target audience. For instance, understanding the target audience helps in the development of marketing strategies to promote your products effectively. A business operating regionally will thus opt for regional advertising channels and creating strong messages that reflect the positioning statement of the business.

The unique positioning of the business requires marketing strategies that identify the products and services in a unique way to the target market. The Audi vehicle manufacturer company, for example, has established itself as a symbol of luxury (Cristea, 2014). The unique positioning of Audi thus, gives potential customers the idea that they will receive luxury products they love from the company. Development of a unique market position will require continuous reinforcement of the target market's perception of the exceptional nature of your products or brand in the market.

Chapter 3
Innovate—Generate and Evaluate

Abstract Chapter three explores the subject of innovation and its impact in the development of businesses. Discussions focused on defining business innovation and its impact on the growth and sustenance of the business entity. Types of innovation are addressed and the innovations process is outlined. The chapter ends with a brief on the challenges to innovation in the Thai context and how to overcome obstacles to innovation to achieve economic development.

3.1 Business Innovation

In business, innovation implies the practice of introducing new ideas, workflows, methods, services, and/or products. The major objective of being innovative in business or an organization is that it is a means of achieving the desired goals within an organization, which are geared towards achieving the aims and initiatives of an organization. The process of innovation is born from the generation of an idea, which is further evaluated in the brainstorming sessions, which considers the viability, durability, and desirability of the concerned idea. Sahut and Peris-Ortiz (2014) indicated that: "Business innovation should either, solve a problem existing in an organization and/or business, improve the quality of existing products or services, or reach to new customers".

The sole purpose of innovation in business is to boost the value of the concerned business or organization. The value is obtained from generation of new revenue opportunities, or making more revenues through already existing channels. This could be achieved through metrics such as saving time, saving money, improving the production process, enhancing performance or advancing the customer's experience. Additionally, as highlighted by Morabito (2017) innovation should lead to improvement in the competitive advantage by helping the concerned organization to grow richer and better, meet and even exceed the set strategic objectives.

Innovation draws on your best practices used by you or your industry and has come to be expected by both consumer and industry. Innovation encompasses many things—development of new products, processes, organizations, management practices and strategies. Changes and improvements in products offered or practices used need to be made periodically. It may come in many different forms—manufacturing processes, delivery systems, new products or data communications and resulting data capture. There is wide agreement that innovation and entrepreneurial activity are the engines of long-run economic growth (Grossman, 1994; Sawmong, 2020b).

The first step to successful innovation management is to choose a strategy. To do that, you must determine if there is a need for an innovation, to what degree and in what areas. This innovation must be one that is clearly understood by all those in the organization whether you are the CEO or the receptionist.

Some firms have found it profitable, as part of their grand strategy to take high initial profits from an improved product or a product that has received wide consumer acceptance. Before the profitability of that product runs out from competition and innovation is replaced by production or marketing performance, a search for new ideas, new products, new improvements or novel ideas must be instituted. The idea is to reinvent or create a new product that will establish a new product cycle for you and basically make the older product no longer useful or out of style.

While innovation of a new product may sound like a good way to beat the competition, care must be taken in the assessment of the end result. The research department of Booz Allen & Hamilton discovered that less than two percent of innovative products developed by 51 companies ever reached the open market. Of 58 new product ideas, only 12 were considered to be acceptable and in line with the firm's long-term objectives and mission. Seven new product ideas remained after initial evaluation of their market potential and only three were actually able to be developed. Assessing the remaining three new products, two showed profit potential after sample test marketing and only one actually made it to commercial success (Booz Allen & Hamilton, 1982).

3.2 Applying the Four Types of Innovation

Whether the business is in its initial start-up stage or it is an established organization, innovation is inevitable, as long as it is planning to remain competitive in the market. Basically, there are two dimensions that as a businessperson you need to consider, the technology and market. Either you are using a new or existing technology, or focusing on new or existing market, it determines the type of innovation to be applied. From the two dimensions, 4 types of innovation are developed, as shown in Fig. 3.1.

3.2.1 Incremental Innovation

This is a type of innovation where you apply the existing technology and focus on increasing the value to the customers (features, design, price, quality etc.) in your exiting market. It is the most common form of innovation in the business world today. It may involve making the products smaller, easier to use, more attractive, or higher in quality or even adjusting the core functionality of the services being offered in the market. It is achieved by increasing efficiency and effectiveness of products and services through constant improvement. A good example is TV, whose it's producer has constantly improved by producing new models while the core idea and components have remained the same.

3.2.2 Disruptive Innovation

This type of innovation is also referred to as stealth innovation. It involves using new technology or techniques on the existing market of the concerned business. It is considered stealthy in nature because the new technology is always considered superior to the existing technology. The characteristics associated with the new technology include having fewer features, more difficult to use, and not authentically pleasing. However, you can use the new technology as a means of providing efficient and more accessible alternatives, as compared to the ones already existing in the market. As a business, the disruptive innovation should be applied to meet the evolving needs, preferences, and tastes of the customers, through development of new value streams that were not there before.

3.2.3 Architectural Innovation

This is a type of innovation, which involves using the existing technology in a new market. Inferring from Morabito (2017), it involves using the existing techniques, processes, and lessons and applying them in a new different market. The main objective of this innovation is increasing the customer's base by focusing on a new market. As a business, your probability of succeeding by applying this technology is quite high because the risk involved is minimal. There is less risk in terms of architectural innovation since the technology being applied is already developed, tested, and proven in the previous market (Perdomo-Ortiz et al., 2006). However, it is important to have the technology tweaking to match the technology with the requirements of the new market.

3.2.4 Radical Innovation

Radical innovation implies the application of new technology in a new market. Practically, this innovation incorporates applying new products, new processes, new services which have high levels of technological advancement and impact is introduced in the new market. It you create a new product or service that was not there in the market previously, and introduce it in the market that you were not operating, then, you are considered to have done radical innovation. It gives birth to new industries and revolutionary technologies.

3.3 The Business Innovation Process

Innovation processes in business aim at increasing the companies' future values. Businesses pursuing successful innovation processes engage in a path of translating new information into desired business solutions. Innovations involve challenges coupled with uncertainty, risk, and complexity; thus, it is critical to developing a systematic structure in the development and implementation of new products (Mitchell & Coles, 2004). The innovation process involves the definition of business ideas in management from the strategic search stage to the last stage of the market launch of the idea. Successful business innovation process can be divided into phases, and each phase has its own characteristics. The development of the innovation process stages differs from business to business, depending on the individual requirements.

3.3.1 Step 1: Idea Generation and Mobilization

The idea generation is the starting line for the business innovation process. New ideas in business are generated from the pressure to compete and to explore the alternative business process to ensure success. Mobilization of new ideas happens when they are moved to new physical and logical locations. Business organizations can promote idea generation through encouraging flexible working conditions and the ability of workers to explore (Geissdoerfer et al., 2017). For example, the Google successfully promotes idea generation through giving autonomy to its employees. Giving the employees autonomy offers them the freedom to define their goals. It encourages job creation leading to the generation of new ideas. New innovative ideas can be in the form of possible new markets, technological solutions, or customer requirements among other ideas.

According to Geissdoerfer et al. (2017), newly generated ideas need different people to move them along. Mobilization ensures that the ideas are passed to different locations. Often, the originators of ideas may not be the marketers of the same ideas, thus other individuals are required to move the ideas along with the innovation phases. Through mobilization, assessment of the ideas is made based on the criteria, potential benefits of the ideas, and feasibility of the ideas to the company. Ideas given priority from this phase based on the assessment criteria are then given priority for the next phase for screening.

3.3.2 Step 2: Advocacy and Screening

Advocacy and screening are the second stage in the business innovation process and it involves weighing the innovative ideas' advantages and disadvantages. The screening of the business innovative ideas is aimed at weeding out ideas that lack potential, while allowing potential ideas to progress in the process. In the second stage, the concepts of the innovative ideas are analyzed based on the goals and expectations of the business allowing potential ideas for further processing. Indeed, not every idea is worth implementing in the business, screening helps determine the ideal decision to be taken, regarding an idea's future in the business.

According to Ciriello et al. (2016), often, most of the innovative idea generators in businesses do not always possess the skills of advocating for their ideas. Advocacy for innovative ideas is thus done by the management working with the innovative employees. The managers can advocate for these ideas by providing facilities, encouragement, and support. Businesses hoping to develop a successful innovation process should build a culture to support idea advocacy and screening. Successful advocacy and screening in business innovation can be achieved through the establishment of enough avenues for advocacy and feedback, as well as the building of transparent screening procedures. The process of advocacy and screening is difficult and every business should be well prepared to ensure success.

3.3.3 Step 3: Experimentation

The third step in the business innovation process involves the experimentation of the concepts developed from the advocacy and screening phase. It is important to understand, that while innovative ideas may have potential benefits to the business, they may be viable in particular business environments or time. Great ideas that are ahead of their time in the markets should not be interpreted as failures but should be used to develop better ideas for particular markets (Frankenberger et al., 2013). The experimentation stage, therefore, tests the suitability of potentially innovative ideas for businesses at particular times. The experimentation process involves testing ideas through "pilot testing" or prototypes. Experimentation of innovation ideas is done on a limited scale to allow for a feasibility study before full-scale implementation. For instance, new ideas in the banking designs can be experimented with within a particular region, using few branches to determine customer response. When the customers respond favorably, then the business can apply the new innovative designs to other branches. Often, the experimentation phase leads to the discovery of new ideas due to the information gathered from the implementation of the original idea.

3.3.4 Step 4: Commercialization

Just like advocacy and screening, the commercialization phase in the business innovation process is vital in ensuring the success of the implementation of new ideas. According to Carayannis et al. (2015), an innovative idea can only be considered an innovation once it is commercialized. The commercialization phase, therefore, involves the creation of the market value for the idea by focusing on the potential impacts. For instance, the business should consider the customer reception towards particular innovations and the analysis of the costs and benefits of commercially rolling out the innovations. Ciriello and Schwabe (2016) informed that the commercialization stage in the innovation process should be refined to meet the needs of the customers. The commercialization of innovation in business involves two phases; the introduction of the innovation and the mass production of the innovation. Successful commercialization of innovations in business requires the establishment of a marketing plan. The marketing plan should be able to increase the innovation's awareness to the customers and increase customer loyalty. An effective marketing strategy will be able to develop a streamlined approach for the successful launch and increase the possibility of the innovation being accepted in the market. Indeed, the commercialization stage involves the various aspects of business and it helps in clarifying the innovative ideas for implementation.

3.3.5 Step 5: Diffusion and Implementation

The last steps in the business innovation process involve the diffusion and implementation processes. Diffusion involves the acceptance of innovative ideas throughout the business organization while the implementation process involves the utilization of innovation. Acceptance of the innovations throughout the company is achieved through the use of knowledge brokers that present the ideas of the innovations to all levels of the organization and consequently aiding in the rapid implementation of the innovations. Implementing innovations is a process that requires resources, strong advocacy, and marketing to the customers (Carayannis, 2015). The diffusion and implementation stage, thus allows the management to determine the required resources to effectively implement the innovations and determining the next set of needs for the customers. Often the diffusion and implementation phase offer the opportunity for the development of future innovative ideas. Similarly, the last phase involves receiving feedback from customers leading to the development of success metrics of the innovations.

3.4 Challenges to Innovation and Support Services in Thailand

Innovation is crucially tied to developments, and implementation of innovation successfully within the framework and operations of SMEs has taken some significance among policymakers, stakeholders, think tanks and government agencies. Some of the main drivers of innovation according to Mahmutaj et al. (2019) are in budgeting, employees' skills, top management support and handling resistance to change by employees'. While the main challenges to innovation were highlighted to include cost-related factors, market conditions, and non-availability of skilled human resources that can foresee and incorporate innovation into the day-to-day operations of the business. The implication of this is the prominence of human skills and the need to invest in technology which is an important innovation driver, and also government policies which in context can help improve or stifle the innovation performance of SMEs.

Thailand as an emerging market has been on a growth trajectory fueled by innovation from the economic successes of the business climate. The Thai government has been focused on continuing economic reforms that are aimed at raising the nation's potential economic progression to attain and maintain high income and inclusive growth. This was proposed in the 20-year national strategy with revamped upscaling in budget disbursement. The major obstacles to innovation have been in the execution of projects notably in the acquisition of land resources and shortages in skilled human resources who have been recognized as the drivers of innovation (Ariyapruchya et al., 2018). Human resources are fundamental because of the linkage role they play in connecting different stakeholders such as government and SMEs, government and international partners (foreign investors). The skill of managing human resources is delicate and requires skilled human interface which has been in short supply.

In healthcare, Innovation is critical to effectively respond to emergencies and plan the economic recovery as was observed during and in the aftermath of the COVID-19 pandemic especially in low and middle-income economies. The need to attract foreign direct investment into the Thai economy is crucial; this ensures that healthcare country managers are proactive and innovative in proposals put forward to address the fallout from such global challenges. Thailand like most emerging economies struggled to contain the outbreak of COVID-19 pandemic, but have recently been able to mitigate the impact because of the innovative approach in dealing with the pandemic and the support of international partners who have collaborated with the Thai government. The biggest challenge facing innovation has been getting the human labor to anticipate and adapt innovation especially those that challenge preexisting sociocultural practices and norms. It is important that such innovation are applied across different sectors for a synergy of the efforts to produce an effect that positively reverberates across the economic sphere of the nation and ensure that future issues can be averted (Kobayashi et al., 2021; Ramalingam & Prabhu, 2020).

Here are some organizations that people looking to do business in Thailand can read about and contact if their values align;

- **The Ministry of Natural Resources and Environment (MONRE)**
  The core MONRE vision is "to return the natural environment to the Thai people and to work towards the incorporation of natural resources and the environment in the Government's national agenda as these provide the basis for social and economic development". The MONRE vision "supports proactive integration of the administrative management of natural resources, environmental protection, and biological diversity, based on the principles of public participation and good governance". Their website is http://www.mnre.go.th/en/about/content/1066.
- **Thai Elephant Conservation**
  A "Mobile Elephant Clinic" with experienced veterinarian that has provided care and health services for elephants in Thailand over the years.
  http://www.phuket.com/conservation/elephants.htm.
- **Thailand Environment Institute Foundation (TEI)**
  The main objectives of TEI are to recommend environmental policy; strengthen capacity in various sectors for managing natural resources; build cooperation with major environmental networks; and campaign to communicate information and knowledge on the environment to society. Their website is http://www.tei.or.th/th/about.php.
- **Smiling Albino**
  Highland Farm & Gibbon Sanctuary Phayathai Babies' Home Clothing, Toys, & Other Stuff English Fun and games for children and adults.
  http://www.smilingalbino.com/community/.
- **Thai Solar Energy Public Company Limited (TSE PCL)**
  TSE PCL is a potential high-impact Thailand industry-based coalition set up in 2008. TSE PCL is the first solar power company in southeastern Asia to "efficiently use state-of-the-art technology to utilize sunlight and convert it into green energy." TSE PCL's vision is to be "a leading regional global provider of renewable energy by means of reliable technologies in order to serve both business and social societies." The mission of TSE PCL is "to establish a solid footprint in Thailand in the solar energy industry and develop a global solar energy business focused on the Asia-Oceania region. Their website is
  http://www.thaisolarenergy.com/profile.php.
- **The Environmental Research Institute Chulalongkorn University**
  The Environmental Research Institute is an important high impact coalition research institute in Thailand. The Environmental Research Institute Chulalongkorn University was established in October 6, 1974. The main mission of this institute is to create knowledge for environmental management and resources that are suitable for countries and regions in Southeast Asia. Their website is http://www.eric.chula.ac.th/administrativeboard.php.

3.4 Challenges to Innovation and Support Services in Thailand

- **Bambi**
  Bambi is a mother-led, non-profit group, offering support and companionship in the early years of parenthood. They hold monthly and weekly playgroups for babies and toddlers. They can be reached at http://www.bambi-bangkok.org/.
- **Computers for Thai Kids**
  The organization has distributed more than 400 computers to government schools across Thailand. They can reached at http://jeep.htmlplanet.com/.
- **Freedom Wheelchairs**
  Foundation to Encourage the Potentially Disabled Persons, located in Chiang Mai, Thailand. They promote and encourage the health, education, employment, and dignity of northern Thailand's disabled persons. More information is available on their website.
     http://disabled.infothai.com/.
- **Thai Chamber of Commerce**.

The Thai Chamber of Commerce is a corporation of organization both local organizations in Thailand with the aim of developing and promoting the interests of Thai local companies and organizations and their relationships with international firms. The members of a Chamber of Commerce are usually local and international operating companies, including lawyers, property developers, tourism firms, airlines, manufacturing companies, import and export companies, banks, finance companies, legal consultants, manufacturers of information technology and electronics. The main activities of the Chambers of Commerce include the protection of business interests, business experiences and business activities. The organizations website can be found at https://thaichamber.org/.

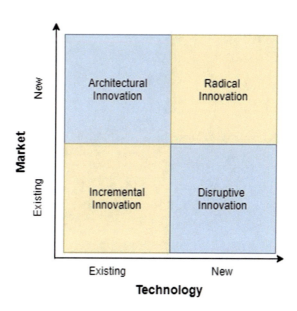

Fig. 3.1 The four types of innovations

Chapter 4
Using Information—Leverage Resource

Abstract The discourse in chapter four centers on the significance of information as an important resource for businesses and how its optimal utility can create value and increase the brand worth to achieve stability and long-term success. The chapter X-rays different forms of information, sources of information and how firms can leverage information to drive revenue. It also discusses the optimal utilization of information in improving operational efficiency and in customer services and research that will give the fir a competitive advantage over its rivals.

4.1 Information as a Resource

You have access to an extensive pool of information and knowledge—whether this is your understanding of customers' needs and the business environment or the skills and experience of your staff. You need to rely on information to make decisions. Even gut feelings, derived from experience can be categorized as a form of internal processing of the business environment. To be competitive in the global market you need to be better positioned and be able to collect and analyze data more effectively. A variety of information must be available to you, such as market research, industry trends, competitor's activity and effective communication skills in dealing with both customer as well as consumer behavior. Information can be collected from trade show attendance, industry specific memberships and affiliations or even your own business systems. ERP (Enterprise Resource Planning) systems allow you to collect data and presentations on all aspects of a business and have a large amount of valuable information at your fingertips. However, this information must be handled properly. You have to remember that other companies may be already using this resource, so you cannot afford to give those other companies any competitive edge. Do not feel comfortable with just basic data. However, keep in mind that companies who are strong market players pay a lot of attention to this part of their operating environment, so to remain competitive you must do the same.

The way you collect, share and utilize this information is critical to your ability to successfully develop. Information management can benefit all sizes of business from a local mom-and-pop operation to an SME to a multinational firm (Belas et al.,

2019; Kotaskova et al., 2020; Meekaewkunchorn et al., 2021; Muangmee et al., 2021), and can be applied to determine the performance of such firms (Wall, 2021a). All businesses have the ability to access wide range of information and knowledge, ranging from the understanding of the customers' needs to comprehending the skills needed in the business environment being operated in. However, Pearlson et al. (2019) observe that the strategies used to gather, share, and exploit the available knowledge is critical in the efforts toward developing a successful business. This is not only beneficial to the large companies, the aspect of information and knowledge management is critical for all businesses, both the local small and medium enterprises as well as large international corporations.

Because of the unique position of Thailand never being colonized by Westerners, the business environment is still dominated by Thai culture that thrives on collectivism. You are expected to share information that is vital for others to survive, a business trend in the Western business world that would instead devalue a competitor rather than sharing information that could be beneficial to them. In the West, the best they do is to buy over such a firm. This would not be the case in a Thai business sector. Knowing the importance of the survival of te business to your rival, and the fact that it is his family means of survival and probably those of the workers employed over there, the objective will be to save the firm rather than let it drown. It takes us back to the principle of "Mai Pen Rai," where Thai people are expected to be content with what they have and exude satisfaction with what they have achieved, and making the most out of any situation they find themselves. This principle has played a critical role in Thailand's development and has seen it stay afloat despite global economic upheavals which have also affect some Southeast Asia nations in recent years.

4.2 Existing Forms of Information

Before starting a business, there are high chances you conducted a market research to evaluate the purpose of your business, or rather, the problem your business will be solving in the market. Actually, this is the first step in developing a business idea, which determines the products or services your business will be offering. This is a form of information about the market that could be tailored as market knowledge regarding customer characteristics and types of products and services. Another form of existing information is held in your files and documents maintained in the business, concerning customers and suppliers. These entities hold a great wealth of information and knowledge, which could be relevant in improving the performance of business through development of new products and services, or improving the existing ones.

Your employees have knowledge, skills, experiences and expertise, which could be exploited as a source of information and knowledge asset. Having employees who are rich in information could be valuable assets that could give you a competitive advantage as compared to your competitors. It is a critical responsibility of the business owners or management to make sure that the knowledge, skills, and information with the current employees are passed to their successors and colleagues whenever possible. This could be achieved through strategies such as training courses and documentations, brainstorming sessions among others.

4.3 Basic Sources of Information

There are various areas that a business should exploit to get business information, and convert it to usable knowledge for the benefit of his/her organization. As a businessperson, you should consider the following sources of business information:

Customer knowledge—this is a source of information, which requires the knowledge of the needs of the customers, and what they think about the business. To tap this information, Vallée (2001) advices that it is important for the business owner to develop a mutually beneficial information and knowledge-sharing relationship, by talking and caring about the future requirements and desires of the customers. And more importantly, business owners should be concerned about their efforts to develop and offer products and services that meet their customers' needs, tastes and preferences.

Employees and Suppliers Relationship—this is gaining information by developing a good relationship with your employees and suppliers. This involves seeking the views of the employees and suppliers. This is because they have their own impressions and observations regarding how you and your business are performing. From their views and propositions, critical information could be obtained.

Market Information—this is where you observe the development and activities occurring in the sector in which your business is operating. The observation should be carried out with a critical eye, asking relevant questions. Some of the questions that should be asked include: How are my competitors performing in the sector? What is the price my competitors are charging for their goods and services? Who are the new entrants in the market? Have any new products or services been launched in the market?

Business Environment—this is searching information regarding the performance of the business you are operating in. Your business could be affected by various factors in the business environment, including development in the political system, the economic changes, technological advancements, society and environmental fluctuations. Therefore, you need to keep yourself informed regarding the development and changes in these areas. It is advisable to set up a team, which could monitor the changes in the business environment, gather relevant information and knowledge and advice the business management accordingly. Sophisticated business process management (BPM) is needed if Thailand's to maintain competitive advantage and meet the business opportunities and overcome challenges from the onset instead of the issues snowballing into a chain reaction, leading to more harmful events capable of derailing positive business directory (Wall et al., 2020).

Professional Associations—this is the practice of creating a positive relationship with the external bodies and organization, to benefit from information and knowledge about them and their activities. These include professional associations, trade unions, conferences, and trade exhibitions. Some sources of critical information include their publications, publications of findings from research bodies, as well as trade and technical magazines. Attending conferences and trade exhibitions could be an effective means of learning about the competitors, the latest innovations, and technological advancement in the market.

Organizational memory—as long as you are concentrating on gaining more and more information, it is crucial to have archives and store relevant information about the business. You should be careful not to lose the information and knowledge and skills that have already been gained by your business. There need to be an explicit way of sharing the employee's information and knowledge for the best ways of doing things.

4.4 Leverage Business Information/Knowledge to Create Value

4.4.1 Leveraging Business Information

Information leverage refers to the use of information data to create value for the business. In the contemporary business environments, it has increasingly become vital for the management and business owners to create, retain, store, disseminate, and reuse information to create a competitive advantage. Businesses with a great understanding of information leverage stand a chance of benefiting from it through improved business results and the development of innovations that will increase the overall business value. In the past, only large organizations were able to invest in big data and were able to leverage the information to create value for their businesses (Côrte-Real et al., 2020). While access to business information has improved over the years, effective leverage of business information requires business organizations to modify their traditional view on information and their information architecture to create business value.

4.4.2 Information in Driving Revenue

Business information can be leveraged to drive revenue through accurate targeting of the customers. Big data information in business gives insights into the target customer trends and behavior vital in helping the businesses to develop accurate ways of interacting with the customers. Information on target audiences in business may highlight behavior such as pain points, shopping behaviors, and why the customers may switch to competitors among other essential customer information. As a business owner, you need to leverage such information by developing solutions to the customer pain points and interacting with the customers to understand their needs and preferences.

According to Côrte-Real et al. (2020), business information can be leveraged to drive top-line revenue by gaining a clear understanding of the customer's journey and improving their experiences in the market. Customers need to gain value for their money. Meeting the customer needs can make the difference in terms of bring competitive advantage in the markets and consequently improving the business' overall revenue income. Similarly, businesses can leverage information to drive revenue through the deployment of data in the business-to-employee (B2E) model. While business information is essential in the alignment of business products to meet customer needs, employees also require extensive information to engage with the customers. The information-rich employees will add value to the business through the rapid and efficient escalation of customer issues thereby improving customer loyalty and consequently improved overall business revenue through sales.

4.4.3 Improving Operational Efficiency

The other way business information can be leveraged to create value is through the improvement of operational efficiencies in business organizations. Improving operational efficiencies affects profitability. Business operations have in the past been impacted by advancements in technology. For instance, companies operating in auto manufacturing benefit from automated operations through robotics. Similarly, the advancements in information computing have developed similar impacts in business operations through the development of predictive analytics, mobile scheduling, and routing among other services (Akter et al., 2016). Businesses can leverage such information to improve their operational efficiencies through the development of systems that can predict equipment lifecycle, and the periods for probable equipment fail to schedule maintenance. The use of predictive analytic in production operations helps in resolving critical operational issues before failure which consequently leads to reduced operational costs and ultimately improved profitability.

Operational efficiency can also be achieved through leveraging information in the supply chains. The big part of business information is ensuring predictive analytics. Supply chains can improve business profitability through control of operating costs. Leveraging business information can be used to control supply chain costs through better forecasting of the inventory used to minimize waste. Information on inventory management permits the generation of reports on inventory use and helps in the development of detailed plans and strategies to minimize wastes and supply chain costs (Akter et al., 2016). For instance, wastes associated with the supply of raw materials such as tomatoes can be analyzed through routine reports on the weather during the harvest time enabling the business to develop storage equipment to minimize wastes through rotting and consequently minimizing operational supply chain costs.

4.4.4 Improving Customer Focus

The concept of customer-centric focus creates business value through increased percentage in profits. Studies by Campbell et al. (2020), indicated high profitability levels of up to 60% for companies with a customer-centric focus. The quest for information regarding customer target is thus vital for many business managers hoping to create value for their organizations through increased profitability. Understanding customer focus is a process involving coordination between the business and the customers. As a business owner, you can leverage information to create customer focus through data collection to create a customer profile. Often customer data collected can be stored in holistic customer profiles to monitor their trends. Information collected from the unified customer profiles is then used in the business-to-customer marketing strategies. The creation of unified customer profiles by the business helps in the correction of information at every touchpoint, including online browsing, mobile interactions, and email clicks regarding their buying journeys. The information is then used in making decisions and strategies such as improving products and services.

In addition, business information can be leveraged to focus on customers through tracking their interactions across data channels. Information channels have been on the increase with the increase in technology. Business owners need to interact with the customers across all channels to create a better understanding of the customer behavior and leveraging the information to create more targeted campaigns. A better understanding of the customer behavior and trends is vital in increased marketing strategies to the target buyers which in turn increases the return on investment (ROI) and consequently creating business value.

4.4.5 Gaining Competitive Advantage

Leveraging business information affects competitive advantage cost and differentiation. Competition in the market continues to get tough as more businesses enter the markets. Business managers understand the importance of seeking core strengths that separate their businesses from the pack in the markets (Grover et al., 2018). Leveraging information offers the opportunity to exploit changes in the competitive scope creating a competitive edge and consequently building business value. Information tools such as Google trends indicate the popularity of products, while social media analytics indicate what the customers think about particular products or services in the market.

4.4 Leverage Business Information/Knowledge to Create Value

According to Pavlou and El Sawy (2006), leveraging information can help your business gain a competitive advantage by exploiting changes in the competitive scope, for instance, information regarding competitive trends in the market may help in the development of differentiation strategies. The aim of using leveraging the information on the competition scope is to keep your eyes on your competitors. Business owners should be concerned about issues such as why the competition is receiving more media coverage and social media trends to ensure that their own business is not being left behind. Leveraging competition information is also vital in determining competitor changes to determine avenues for exploitation. For instance, where the information in the market indicates that other competitors are doing better than you, decisions to increase marketing campaigns should be made as well as product differentiation to gain a competitive edge and consequently creating business value.

4.4.6 Setting Realistic Goals

Decision-makers in the organization play vital roles in the growth and development of the business. Often decision-makers rely on intuition and experience to make valuable decisions. While using intuition and experience in decision-making are important, it is also beneficial to rely on data in affecting business decisions (He et al., 2017). Decisions regarding business goals require the right information to set the business on the right path for future success. Leveraging information in the setting of realistic business goals is vital to avoid the scenario of shifting goals from time to time. Leveraging information during the setting of business goals involves the use of historical trends and activities in the same market to ensure clear goals from the start.

Analyzing historical data on the business activities in the market enables you to understand the weaknesses and strengths of the business. This enables you to know areas you need to improve on to grow the business and where you are doing well already and sustain your efforts thereby creating value. Similarly, clear and realistic business goals based on data analysis often make it clear when certain goals are not possible, thereby helping the decision-makers to concentrate their resources on productive goals to increase business growth (He et al., 2017). Realistic goals affect the strategic decisions in the business in the long term. For instance, making good decisions on pricing strategies and inventory management can only be achieved through clear analysis of historical business data on similar activities. Businesses relying upon leveraging data are likely to report improved growth due to realistic business goals and better decision making.

Chapter 5
Technology—Upgrade

Abstract This chapter introduces the topic that discusses upgrade of technology and how it can be applied successfully in business. It buttresses loopholes that need to be identified when working with technology. It also stresses the importance of pilot operations to test the efficacy of the proposed technology, the communication plan that outlines modalities of the technology, training for staff before deployment, infrastructure and technical support, integrity of the technology and its security, as well as reviewing its performance and possible upgrades as they may be required to account of changing data and societal behavior.

5.1 Technology in Business

The manufacture and delivery or goods and/or services are a major area of concern for a globally competitive company. If entry barriers protect a domestic company from imports then the need for technology and subsequent upgrades can be minimal. Old equipment can continue to be used along with inefficient processes far beyond their projected useful life and consumers are therefore subjected to status quo efficiency with limited or no product choice, but that is not the real world for the majority of companies and their customers.

Today, you must constantly assess how you produce and deliver products, offer services and keep track of data on the consumer and the competition. Upgrading, however, can be expensive. The pitfall is that in an effort to possess the latest and the greatest technology to stay ahead of the competition, you can find yourself carrying heavy debt loads to finance this technology which the product or service may not be able to support. You must make careful assessment before technological upgrades are ordered and decisions are made for major improvement.

Using a simple question and answer format, can help with your technology assessment process:

- Research technical upgrades, analyze and evaluate reasons and prioritize what those upgrade goals are.
- Analyze the savings and benefits, both short term and long term, on the product and/or service.

- Estimate upgrade costs and related savings on production
- Consider:
  - equipment costs
  - maintenance costs
  - installation costs
  - other cost factors
- Assess the scope of work necessary to upgrade and consider:
  - technical complexities
  - compatibility issues
  - extra work hours
  - scheduling
  - other factors
- Reassess and justify any major or minor informed upgrade decisions.
- For planning in the future, document and keep all records of the upgrade analysis process as well as all lessons learned from your assessment process.

5.2 Steps to Follow When Upgrading Your Business Technology

Technology is constantly evolving, and this leaves many businesses in a dilemma on the right time to upgrade to new business technologies. Every business aims to maximize revenue; thus, any technological upgrade will only make sense if it will help your company to grow in revenue and achieve overall business success. As a business manager, various signs will indicate that your business is in of technological upgrades. For instance, where your company is growing rapidly, drastic changes need to be made to technology to better manage the possible additional departments and new employees. In addition, where the business indicates a clear problem, then upgrades in technology may be necessary to solve the underlying issues. In this case, however, the process of upgrading should be based on the understanding of the business needs by the managers and the employees. Once you have made the decision to upgrade your business technology, there is a need to follow a step-by-step process to ensure technological upgrade implementation is successful.

5.2.1 Step 1: Identify Technological Loopholes

The need for the installation of technology in business is to solve problems. The decision to upgrade the business' technology should thus solve the existing problems in the business. While shopping for new technology, you need to identify exactly what is not working in your organization. Existing technology should be analyzed on why it is not working. For example, you should analyze why the existing technology is not working based on resource allocation, talent, and the obsolete nature of the technology. According to du Toit (2019), consulting with the organization's IT department will be vital in understanding the required technological upgrades and will help save costly mistakes of purchasing new incompatible technology. Your IT department stays up to date with the existing technologies in the business and has a better understanding of what will be compatible during the upgrade. Identification of technological loopholes should also involve other stakeholders in the business, including employees and managers at all levels using the existing technologies. Involving all stakeholders from all levels will help identify the unexpected problems that crop up during the technological upgrade process (Chaveesuk et al., 2020).

5.2.2 Step 2: Pilot Operation

The next step in the upgrading of business technology is to run a pilot operation of the chosen technology. There are various technologies that can be used in solving business operations, however, as a manager, you should choose the most appropriate technology, which is compatible with your business model and is cost-effective. Running a pilot operation of the chosen technologies thus involves selecting a small segment within the business to test the new technology. Running a pilot operation will help your business to minimize risk, in case the technology is not successfully implemented. Also, the pilot program helps in working out any kinks that may arise before full-scale implementation of the programs (Kamariotou & Kitsios, 2017). An example may be a business hoping to install the new Microsoft office 365 in its operations. The pilot program will thus involve doing a free trial of the program for thirty days before the company decides on the package it would purchase for its technological upgrade. After any possible challenges in the implementation of the new technology have been ironed out, you can now move to the other stages in the implementation of a technology upgrade to your business.

5.2.3 Step 3: Communication Plan

Technologies used by business organizations serve a wide range of persons, including internal employees and external vendors and customers. Any plans to upgrade your business technologies will thus need to take into account how the changes will affect the stakeholders in your business. The communication plan should be put in place to inform the stakeholders of the proposed technological changes and allow them time to adjust to the new programs. For instance, communication regarding changes in the business' technology should be sent to all stakeholders at least a month before the proposed changes. As a manager, your communication on business technology upgrade should include information on how the changes will affect the internal department's operations and how to use the new products. Also, the communications should inform the customers on the new ways of interaction based on the new technology. An effective communication plan will help eliminate any form of confusion that may arise from the technological upgrades and reduce downtime of access from the external stakeholders such as vendors.

5.2.4 Step 4: Training

Often, some upgrades in business technology are complicated and may lead to the complete change of the product. As a business manager, you need to answer the question, what good is new technology if the employees are not able to use it? Installation of technological upgrades may lead to unprecedented growth or decline depending on the utilization of the new technological resources. Effective training on the use of the newly upgraded technologies is vital in ensuring faster adaptation by the staff and reducing downtimes. Training, therefore, makes the implementation of new technologies easier and user friendly by reducing any complexities associated with the new upgrades. While providing training, you should consider various aspects that will ensure effective training of the employees. For instance, you should ensure the training is done using different learning styles and needs. Tailored training sessions ensure that all types of learners among the employees are adequately informed. Similarly, the training program should include employee feedback from every department to determine the adoption rates of the new technology upgrades in the business.

5.2.5 Step 5: Preparing Infrastructure

Business technology upgrades often introduce significant changes to the operations procedures. Often purchasing new technologies may lead to a possible increase in production or an influx in data that may prove difficult for the current team to manage with the existing infrastructure. To avoid the possible chaos in management due to new technological upgrades, it is advisable for you to take stock of the existing infrastructure and prepare the adequate infrastructure to accommodate the expected changes. For instance, upgrading the marketing computing analytics software will result in the analysis large of marketing data. Preparing infrastructure, in this case, will thus require your business to invest in data collection infrastructure such as the purchase of computer hardware used in data storage.

5.2.6 Step 6: Implementation and Support

Making it to the implementation stage means you have analyzed and fine-tuned the new business technologies. The implementation process may involve moving from one department to another or full implementation in all departments at the same time. However, the installation of new technologies is not always smooth and may be marred by various vulnerabilities. Your business technology upgrade implementation phase should therefore include contingency plans to support the new technologies' post-implementation. For instance, some technologies take a while for problems to arise after implementation. Technological upgrade support in business, therefore, involves the stage of ensuring success in the integration of the new technologies. According to Ghobakhloo (2020), your technology upgrade implementation plan should take into account the risks involved in the running of the technologies before they are fully integrated into the business operations. Often, supporting new technologies may include plans to keep the technologies running in case of power outages, or cyber-attacks. As a manager, you can promote post-implementation support by developing open channels for support. For example, employees finding challenges in operating the newly upgraded technologies should be readily assisted by their managers to ensure smooth integration of the new technologies.

5.2.7 Step 7: Performing Upgrade Review

After the implementation of the business technology upgrades, it is essential to review the projects to identify what worked well and areas that may require improvement to ensure an effective technology upgrade implementation process. Performing an upgrade review after implementation will help you keep documentation of the process that can be used during the next of implanting new technologies. Technological changes are occurring at an incredible rate and making mistakes may be costly to the overall business success. Reviews of technological upgrades offer you the opportunity of not making the same mistakes again on processes that did not work during the previous technological upgrades in your business. According to Radosevic and Yoruk (2016), even the best-laid plans run the risk of going awry, however, having a well-thought-out plan could make the implementation of the new technologies smooth.

5.3 Benefits of Upgrading Technology in Business

Technology in business plays a vital role in operational efficiency and ensuring customer satisfaction among other benefits. Therefore, managing a solid technological infrastructure in the business comes with the benefits of smooth business operations, efficient transactions, and reduced operations costs. However, running an out-of-date technological system will not only hold back your business, but will also expose the business to security risks such as cyber-attacks. This may lead to reduced productivity and consequently decline in overall business performance. The increasing advancement in technology may lead to a question such as: when is the right time to upgrade my business technologies? There is no specific timeline used to update the business technologies, and it all depends on the size and nature of the business you are running. There are various benefits of upgrading your business technologies. Some these benefits are explained below.

5.3.1 Increased Productivity

Using technology in business helps in driving productivity and growth through increased engagement of the employees. Communication technologies support increased coordination among the workers thereby reducing time wastage and increasing productivity. However, using outdated technologies may lead to limitations in productivity levels. For instance, a business using outdated computer hardware desktops or laptops will demoralize the workers and may limit productivity rates. According to Venkitachalam and Ambrosini (2017), using old computers and outdated operating systems decreases the productivity levels of a business by up to 30%. Similarly, remote working has become a developing feature since the outbreak of the COVID-19 pandemic. Upgrading the technology thus will offer your employees more flexibility and functionality that will increase their daily productivity even when working remotely. Adequate technology upgrade including updated operating systems and up to date computers will ensure you maintain the same level of communication needed for feedback as is the case in the normal office environment.

5.3.2 Security of Data

Business information has increased its importance over the years and may determine the business' competitive edge. Thus, in your business, keeping secure the business data is vital in maintaining the competitive advantage in the market. Competition in the business world has become stiff and any mistake may lead to losing the market advantage. Often, hackers try to infiltrate the business' systems to steal data aimed at damaging the reputation of the business or to make money out of selling the data to your competitors (Praveena and Smys, 2017). Old and outdated technological systems are vulnerable to infiltration where viruses and malware may make it hard for the business to function. Updating the business' technological systems will include the installation of newer security functions that will be difficult to hack and will ensure the protection of your business data against attacks.

5.3.3 Attracting More Customers

The use of technology has changed the way people shop. The increased use of mobile smartphone technologies has increased online shopping and the way customers perceive businesses. A study by Groß (2015), indicate that 50% of smartphone users search products online, and nine out of ten searches end in a purchase. A great number of young shoppers rarely visit the physical business locations to make their purchases instead they order the products they need through their mobile devices to be delivered to their locations. Attracting these customers thus requires upgrading your business to accommodate smartphone users. For example, you can upgrade your business by optimizing the business website for mobile use. Similarly, you can develop a mobile phone app to enable smartphone users to access your business and consequently increase your customer base.

5.3.4 Cost Minimization

Technological changes are inevitable as technology is always changing. It is thus common for old technologies to wear out as the technologies they use become obsolete in the market operations. Sometimes, as a business owner, you may realize that one of the things costing you money is sticking with the old technologies. For instance, using old technologies may necessitate constant repair, which increases the costs of operations. Upgrading to new systems may thus be a form of cost minimization, as some of the new technological gadgets have been developed to be cost-efficient such as being energy efficient. Similarly, change is constant, and trying to keep up with the technological changes may be costly for your business. Upgrading the existing technologies is a cheap way of operating using up-to-date technologies.

5.3.5 Solving Problems

The greatest reason for incorporating technology in business operations is to find solutions for underlying business problems. For example, if your company has communication problems. Developing a secure communication channel using technology can help ease such problems, thereby increasing coordination and consequently overall productivity. Different business technologies come with different problem-solving capabilities. For instance, a business hoping to integrate its departments to enable effective decision-making may require upgrading its ERP systems (Barth & Koch, 2019). Installing some technological systems may be costly in the beginning, but will prove to be beneficial in the long run. In case your current technologies do not support the desired growth in your business, making changes through upgrading the technologies may prove to be beneficial in the long run.

5.4 Technology Transfer/Access to Technology

The paper by Sripaipan (1991) chronicles the evolution of science and technology in Thailand and the different stages through its development and agencies involved in the regulation of technology. Technology transfer is built around funding of Research and Development (R&D) units in organizations. However, most Thai firms have been found to rely mostly on existing technology instead of investing in new technology initiatives that will broaden the horizon of technology towards innovations that will improve society. New technologies have been known to arouse optimism and anxiety simultaneously, leading to what Servaes (1990) describes as the opposite "boom" versus "doom" situation. Gibson and Smilor (1991) identified technology transfer as a frequently anarchic, disordered process that involves individuals and groups may have divergent opinions regarding the significance and potential usefulness of the technology. They stated that technology itself is often times not ascribed any absolute denotation or value.

Chung (2001) considers technology transfer as the transmission of knowledge and expertise to suit local settings, with efficient incorporation and transmission both within and beyond the borders of a nation. Autio and Laamanen (1995) provide a broader context by suggesting that technology transfer is intentional, objective-focused interface between two or more individuals or groups, through which the assemblage of technological know-how are kept stable or increased via the transfer of one or more constituents of technology. The process of technological transfer is not built only on the concept of transmitting technology from one entity to another, but also on the capability of the receiving entity to absorb, process and utilize the technology it is receiving. Based on this concept, the process of technology transfer can be viewed from two dimensions, production of a new product and secondly, the enhancement of an already existing product towards making its performance optimal (Das, 1987). Depending on the industry, these technologies abound both the new and improved versions of technologies. The technology producers are usually the western nations and receivers are mostly the developing low-income and middle-income nations of which Thailand is among.

5.4.1 Barriers to Technological Transfer

Barriers to technological transfer can be broadly classified into domestic and external barriers. They can be considered from the point of view of recipient/supplier or in the context of international relations. Domestic barriers in Thailand could come in the form of infrastructural deficiencies, lack of skilled manpower, poor inter-government agency cooperation, and poor information network and database systems especially technical information. Some of these deficiencies were exposed critically during the outbreak of the COVID-19 pandemic; most government agencies were struggling with the scope of infections showing an apparent lack of technological know-how

5.4 Technology Transfer/Access to Technology

to manage the fallout of the pandemic. It is paramount to frequently update and distribute technical information to the related agencies, stakeholders and the public. A regular update of information requires highly trained personnel in information management and a good international communication background.

The key point to note is that internal barriers to technological transfer deter national development of capacity building and technological transfer. The private sector also have an important role to play in technological transfer, unfortunately, they are less motivated because of the huge costs involved in acquiring technology and the need for them to make profit, which is overriding above any other interest. It is challenging to foresee a transfer of high cost advanced technology without public policy support. Technology transfer is too crucial to be dependent on profit as a motivation for their acquisition. Some technology may not make profit for people who adopt them, but are critical because of the value they add to the advancement of humans.

External barriers are regarded as more significant to beneficial technological transfer. Because developed nations are mostly the suppliers of these innovative technologies, and there is a big likelihood of them sending outdated or unsuitable versions of technologies that do not take into account the local vagaries of the recipient country. To forestall such predicaments, nations that have or intend to have external technological transfer with supplier nations should a strong binding agreement that specify exact deliverables to recipient nations. To avert shortage of skilled manpower to operate, maintain and regulate such technologies, agreements must include capacity training of nationals from the recipient nation so they can handle technical challenges arising from the glitches from the use of the technology as more variables are introduced into the system. This instance is of particular interest to Thailand that is mostly a recipient nation, sufficient information should be made available to ensure the country chooses the appropriate technology that will work under the dictates of the cultural, political and socioeconomic conditions of the country.

Sripaipan (1991) suggested strategies that are to be implemented for a successful technological transfer and what is required of countries to realize such strategies:

- Assist and inspire private sector participation in the nationwide adoption of technology in business operations through enabling a competitive environment by providing fiscal incentives to motivate firms at the forefront of R&D in technology transfer.
- Government agencies should ensure that information on available technology is disseminated to the sectors concerned and make regulations to boost the development of precise technology for specific industries.
- Advance the adoption of modern technological tools and management to enhance output, lower costs through stabilized pricing of mechanized agricultural tools and encourage cooperation among farmers, furthering extension services to reach inaccessible rural farmers, and amplify the role of the private sector in technology transfer .

- Enhance the effectiveness of acquisition and transfer of technology to reinforce bargaining power, promote the dissemination of imported technology, upgrade the technological infrastructure and capability of government agencies, and oversee large scale technology transfer initiatives.

Chapter 6
Human Resources/Cross-cultural Communication—Breed Success

Abstract This chapter discusses the relevance of human resources and the interconnection with cross-cultural communication. It highlights the role of human resources management communication in the business objectives. It also makes emphasis on how strategic communication can benefit any organization, its functional implementation, benefits and risks associated with such a communication strategy. Overall, it does justice to discussion on human resources as a business asset, human capital, and its contribution to the viability of an organization. The communication culture of an organization is a function of its human resources unit, and the interactions lead to cross-cultural effect that can be harnessed to benefit the business entity or organization.

6.1 Human Resource Development

What you need most importantly to facilitate operational methods and the processes of operation are trained, skilled employees. You need to be able to be supported by a strong educational base that provides graduates with a strong curriculum that is based on the real demands of business today. Education today has migrated online therefore extending the reach of learning beyond the walls of an educational institution (Khalid et al., 2021), this is more so with the outbreak of COVID-19 pandemic (Khalid et al., 2021). Employees no longer have a reason for non-capacity development. Successful companies will tell you that a large part of their success is attributable to their employees. Valued employees are a successful company's most valued asset and these companies invest large amounts of time, money and other resources to properly train and retain them. Successful companies always have an easier time attracting the best people and you must do the same. Success breeds success. Companies need to have programs in place that will attract the best people in their business. You need to attract the best people but cannot expect to keep them if they have no programs in place. One of such programs is Employee stock ownership plans (ESOP). ESOP involves encouraging company ownership by employees, bringing commitment and a level of pride to employees to strive for success and therefore creates a win–win relationship between you and your employee.

"The manager is the dynamic, life-giving element in every business" according to Peter Drucker in his 1993 book *The Practice of Management*. While this may hold true in a strictly top-down form of management, many business firms rely on teamwork and employee and also believe that customer feedback is critical to being competitive.

In a globally competitive situation, you need to assess your ability to succeed in global management. You need to make yourself (or your multicultural team) more effective. You must pay close attention to skills needed to succeed in a culturally diverse environment.

Some of those issues include a self-knowledge to understand your own cultural values and how they affect your behavior and attitudes. You need to stay informed about global events especially in those areas that you are or plan to market to. Cultural behaviors of others must be looked at in a non-judgmental way. In the same way, you need to be flexible and be able to adapt to a variety of operational practices, business styles and social environments, making people from different backgrounds feel relaxed and comfortable, understood and valued for their perspectives.

Interpersonal communication skills must allow you to express yourself persuasively while listening genuinely to hear what others are saying to you. In this way, you will inspire your employees or team to take responsibility and be initiators, to collaborate and contribute the creativity of their differences. All of these skills will take patience and you need patience to work with other people's needs and schedules, as well as in focusing on long-term goals, without wasting time on goodwill in order to get immediate results.

6.2 Cross-cultural Communication Awareness

A major challenge for a company competing in the global marketplace is their integration and understanding of the wide cultural diversity that is encountered when producing a product, offering a service and communicating with customers. Products and/or services that address specific cross-cultural requirements of customers need to be considered. To this end, cross-cultural communication is a necessity today for staying competitive and attracting a broad base of customers.

Cultural backgrounds and behavior are exhibited in some ways that are obvious and others that are very subtle. Things like appearance, names, language, and accents are all visible and quite apparent. Less apparent are attitudes toward time, commitments, success, status, authority, planning, negotiation, teamwork, personal boundaries and body language and social interactions.

Some of the most frequently encountered cultural issues are listed and explained within the text that follows.

Verbal or Visual cultural backgrounds and behavior deals primarily with the following issues:

6.2 Cross-cultural Communication Awareness

- Appearance
- Names
- Language
- Accents

Non-Verbal cultural backgrounds and behavior can take many forms and need a higher degree of skill level to perceive and understand. These are such things as:

- Commitments
- Success
- Status
- Authority
- Planning
- Negotiation
- Teamwork
- Personal boundaries
- Social Interaction
- Time [Interact effectively with people who seem to have a completely different sense of time].

Beyond the actual product and/or service provided, employees of your company must always be adequately prepared to deal with cross-cultural issues and be able to communicate effectively while dealing with the nuances of a global population. They must be capable of more than just effectively communicating verbal information in a customer's native language. To be a truly valuable resource to your company's success, you must also be able to recognize these signals from the customer in their reaction to a product and/or service.

6.3 Focusing HRM Communication Towards Business Missions

Communication is a vital aspect in every business and the human resource management component can utilize it to breed success in business organizations. As a human resource manager, contributing to the business overall success included learning how to effectively communicate with the employees. The HRM department communicates with employees on various levels, focusing these communications towards the business' mission, and vision will lead to a more focused workforce and increased overall productivity (Schiemann et al., 2018). There are various ways that you can utilize HRM to communicate the business mission.

6.3.1 Strategic Communication

The HRM department is among those responsible for defining the organization's strategic growth strategies. Businesses design mission statements that are aimed at ensuring increased productivity and business success. Top HRM management thus has the opportunity to communicate strategic HR guidelines that will ensure creation of productive and engaged workforce to ensure business success (Van Mierlo, 2018). As a top human resources manager, you can strategically communicate the return-on-investment HR activities with the top management by linking them to the business mission and ensuring overall business success.

6.3.2 Communicating Human Resources Benefits and Risks

Employees play an important role in business success, these ranges from production to being the face of the business. Effective handling of the employee's affairs may determine the deference between business success and failure. As a manager, effective communication through the HR leadership is vital in minimizing the liabilities that may arise from the company's unfair employee relations. Unfair treatment of employees may lead to disgruntled employees and consequently lead to liabilities in form of lawsuits, and declined productivity. Communicating effective human resource practices based on the business's mission will lead to increased productivity and bring about overall success of your business.

6.3.3 Functional Implementation

The HRM function in business can also focus the communication on the business mission through demonstration of the best HR practices in the organizational operations. Ensuring functional implementation of HRM practices in your business may include communicating to the human resource staff on how best to serve the needs of the employees towards the attainment of the business mission and goals (Al-Sarayrah et al., 2016). For instance, communicating the understanding that the employees are the business' internal customers will effectively align the HR practices with the business' strategic goals.

6.4 Creating Effective Communication Within the Organization

Organizational communication entails formal and informal communication in the organization involving the employees and the management. Communications in an organization may be in various ways, including; communication to employees, with employees and from employees to the management. Creating a comprehensive communication strategy helps in the ensuing communication of consistent messages as well as affective delivery of messages from the top management with elaborate organizational mission, vision and culture (Gochhayat et al., 2017). Creating effective communication within the organization will thus be a big leap into the maximization of employee performance and overall business success.

Successful organizations employ various communication strategies to achieve efficiency. Creating an open communication environment is one way of building trust and ensuring effective communication within an organization. As a manager, creating an open communication environment will help your employees to be free to share any interesting ideas on organizational issues as well as criticize any issues that may hinder performance. It is also advisable to ensure that the organization's communication procedure is two-way. Two-way communication process occurs either in the vertical or horizontal communication process and this allows even the workers at lower levels to transfer information to other senior employees. Other ways you can create an effective communication within an organization may include encouraging feedback from the workers on organizational operations to demonstrate that their opinions matter and focusing on listening when interacting on the one-on-one basis with the employees.

Effective communication in the organization should be the target of every manager as it contributes to the overall success of the organization. Effective communication is your organization will positively impact the employees by boosting their morale, fostering job satisfaction and engagement in organizational operations. Creating an open communication environment, for instance, offers the employees a voice to air their opinions and criticisms where necessary concerning the operations of the organization and consequently improving the employee satisfaction.

6.5 Human Resource as a Business Asset

Human resources in business organization have proved to be intangible assets in the business. Indeed, often, employees leaving an organization may be replaced physically; however, their skill sets and knowledge may prove a challenge to replace. According to Al-Sarayrah et al. (2016), the employee skills account for three-quarter of the company's assets, and their efficiency determines the success rate in any business. Thus, like other assets in the business, your company's human resources comprising the employees can be used to produce earnings and form an important resource in the business. There are various ways your business can use the human resources as assets that will drive the success of the organization.

6.5.1 Human Capital

Considering the human resources as human capital indicates that the employees are viewed as assets and not costs. Every business aims to maximize its capital efficiency while minimizing costs. Consequently, in managing your human resources as assets, you need to maximize their efficiency through employee protection (Merriman, 2017). Protecting your workforce as business assets involves understanding the employees' priorities and to ensure that their needs are met. Managing employees in a manner that indicate that they are expendable will lead to a decline in employee morale and productivity, consequently turning into costs.

6.5.2 Possess Skills and Knowledge

Every business maintains assets that cannot be matched by their competitors to maintain their competitive advantage. Similarly, the human resources in your business possess particular skills and knowledge in specific areas of the business's operations and an understanding of the business culture. Managing your employees as the business' assets safeguards the skills and knowledge of your company's operations that may be difficult to operate (Merriman, 2017). Safeguarding your human resource's skills and protection knowledge thus helps in improving efficiency and maintaining the competitive advantage for business success.

6.5.3 Contribution to Profits

Business assets contribute to the overall business profits and worth. The business' human resources contribute to profits in many ways and are consequently considered as assets. Employees in your business offer commitment and dedication, resulting to business success. The view of the employees as valuable employees therefore should involve managing their needs to improve their efficiency and productivity. For example, improving the remuneration will improve employee motivation and will result in improved productivity and success of the organization.

6.6 Creating Company Culture that Breeds Success

Organizational culture involves shared beliefs that support the company's strategy and structure. A company with a strong organizational culture benefits through the employees' understanding of the management needs, and an understanding of the company values and the expected responses. Multinational organizations are often exposed to different national cultures in their areas of operation. Creating an organizational culture therefore will help your organization to set particular expectations for the employees on how to behave and work as a team to achieve the organization's set goals.

The strongest organizational culture is based on values of human nature, the organization's relations with its environment, appropriate emotions and effectiveness. Thus, creating your organization's company culture will involve the laying the foundation to fuse the culture with the values. According to Tosti (2007) creating company culture takes time and aligning them with your company's mission, vision, and values will help your employees to take time and effort to realize these values. For example, if your company seeks excellence through innovation and integrity, then the values should be part of the company's hiring process and the business operations. Similarly, you can create company culture through engaging the employees. Employees play a vital role in productivity, thus incorporating their culture would be a good start to creating the organizations' culture. Engaging the employees can be achieved through conducting of regular culture surveys.

Creating a strong company culture will benefit the organization through improved brand reputation. Often, the way the community views your business has the power to improve your brand recognition and consequently improved business success. Positive brand recognition will make more customers want to patronize your business (Al-Alawi et al., 2007). Similarly, creating a strong company culture can breed success through increased employee retention and improved productivity. Incorporating the employees' opinions in the development of your company's culture will build a happier workforce and lead to increase in productivity. More workers are likely to show up consistently and are likely to take up fewer sick leaves. This will boost productivity and overall success of the business.

6.7 Developing Cross-cultural Communication

The increased globalization in the markets has led to increased diversity in many workplaces and other business shareholders. Organizations conducting global business need to understand the complexities of cross-cultural communication in the workplaces to ensure success. As McLean (2010) observes, cross-cultural communication presents an understanding of how different persons from different cultures communicate, and perceive their business environments. For instance, silence between a question during business communication may be considered a sign of good listening skill in the Asian culture, while it may be viewed as an awkward moment in the American culture. Developing a cross-cultural communication strategy is thus critical in ensuring business success.

Increasing diversity awareness is one of the steps towards developing cross-cultural communication in your organization to breed success. As a human resources manager, creating diversity awareness involves the understanding that different employees come from different ethnic and cultural backgrounds and they may interpret different communications in different ways. For instance, the use of particular slang in an organization may be harmful in some cultures where the language may convey hatred. Similarly, cross-cultural communication can be encouraged to promote business success through strengthening of individual culture knowledge. There are different diverse cultures and it may be difficult to know when to communicate appropriately to your employees or customers. Thus, training your supervisors to understand the different cultural interactions will be vital in improving the cross-cultural communication process and consequently increasing organizational success. For instance, supervisors with good understanding of the different cultural interactions will be more sensitive to the different ways of interacting with employees.

Developing a cross-cultural communication process in your organization comes with the benefits of building trust between the management and the employees. Respecting the different cultures is vital in establishing an efficient working relationship among the employees, and this is a necessary condition for success in business. Enhanced cross-cultural communication also helps in improving the quality of communication within the organization (Wall, 2021b). The top management is able to deliver its message concerning its mission, vision and values effectively. This encourages understanding of organizational goals, and teamwork thereby improving productivity. Also, employee morale can be improved through enhanced cross-cultural communication. Employees from different cultures will feel appreciated and are likely to increase their productivity levels.

6.8 Developing of Cultural Intelligence

Apart from communicating cultural differences in business operations, developing a high cultural intelligence among the employees creates a competitive advantage for the business leading to unprecedented success in the global markets. It is also an indication of high performance in a new culture. For businesses operating in overseas markets, the human resource may play a vital role in accelerating the development of cultural intelligence among the employees through training.

Establishing a global mindset is one of the ways you can use to develop cultural intelligence among your employees. A global mindset entails approaching the cross-cultural work with an open mindset. Developing a cultural intelligence entails training the workforce to work effectively with different groups from different cultures to achieve the set business goals and mission. Achieving these goals is vital in breaking operational bias in all levels of the business and preventing any form of wrong assumptions that may be culturally inappropriate. According to Setti et al. (2020), there are various ways of raising the cultural intelligence among the employees. For instance, creating an enabling environment to learn about other cultures will motivate the workers to know more about cultures alien to their environment. Similarly, communication situations arising from the inappropriateness of one's culture may serve as learning outcomes about other people's culture, providing an avenue for further learning and unlearning, thus improving their cultural intelligence through contact with other cultures and value system.

Expatiating on the cultural intelligence of Thailand, the Thai society is styled as collective, cohesive, free and open environment, which has the country remain a top tourist destination over the years. The societal values has seen it as one of the most alluring and captivating places to visit and conduct business globally. The cultural values are underpinned by Buddhism is the faith which is practiced by about 95 percent of the Thai population. Thai people share a rich ethnic and cultural diversity with the Tai, Khmer, Laotian, Chinese, Mon, Indian and Malay, this blend has resulted in no one laying claim to be 100% Thai. More than 80% of all Thais are in some way connected with agriculture, whose influence can be seen in cultural festivals and religious ceremonies which add to the distinctiveness of Thailand as a free and culture-rich nation. Payutto (2003) contextualizes that the influence of Buddhism permeates the Thai culture and its principles are enshrined in the Thai society. This is observable in the teachings where great emphasis is placed abhorring vices like hatred, greed, lust, delusion and self-gain. The teachings of Buddhism counters these vices with the right information and knowledge about self and the community, with knowledge, it the mind will be equipped to make the right choices and understand that greed and accumulation of wealth are meaningless as they have no significance here or in the hereafter, religious tenets are prioritized instead.

The postulates of Thomas and Inkson (2004, 2005, 2006), three characteristics are tied to the acquisition of cultural intelligence; they are integrity, openness and hardiness. They buttress that integrity involves the attainment of a finely honed sense of self and a thorough understanding of how one's own belief and value system influences human behavior. Openness according to them involves demonstrating reverence and courteousness when engaging with others and at the same time revealing a desire to inculcate values from them. They viewed hardiness as sturdiness, valor, fearlessness, and the ability to survive inclement situations whether natural or man-made. The correlation of the three characteristics that enhance cultural intelligence has a close affinity with Buddha's main teachings. Juxtaposing this with the traditional Thai society, the observations are not too far from what is obtainable. Buddha's core tenets instructs adherents to always do good in the society, encourage them to help others as much as possible, sympathize and empathize with those in need and undergoing adversity, and support the society within their means. The teachings of Buddha encourage the development of human resources, and it begins with self-development, self-training including the physical aspect and through mentors. The teaching enjoins that those who develop themselves are likely to gain more cultural intelligence over those who abstain from self-development.

Chapter 7
Strategic Alliance—Strength in Numbers

Abstract Strategic alliance is beneficial to businesses. From historical contexts, evidence abound of how strategic alliance turned the tide of great battles, so also, this is applicable in running businesses. Having the right alliance can make a huge difference between profit and losses, or the liquidity of a business entity. This chapter discusses advantages and disadvantages of alliances, and how alliances can be leveraged to build trust and gaining new insights in business. Types of alliances are also addressed, things to consider if an alliance is to be successful, and ensuring the right agreement that is favorable to both the organization and its strategic allies.

7.1 The Spirit of Strategic Alliance

Whether we call it 'symbiotic relationship' the 'search for synergies' or simply creation of 'strategic alliance' it is evident that there is strength in numbers. No business enterprise or firm could be considered an "expert" in all areas of business functionality. However, it is vital for all business to master the core operational areas such as producing, packaging, distributing, logistics, marketing and advertising, and human resource. According to Nguyen and Tran (2019), the complexity of business and the inevitable and new-found spirit of sharing has led to the development and adoption of the spirit of 'strategic alliance'.

Survive together, die alone. Partners working together can achieve more success through an effective company alliance. Sometimes this type of alliance can be very beneficial for a company. A smaller company may benefit from an alliance with a stronger partner. A good example of this is providing anything from a simple distribution arrangement of a product to being a source of production, which could be very beneficial if, for instance, you are looking to export a product. Using local expertise in your target market could be a direct benefit to you rather than having to develop your own expertise in that same market. Better purchasing power and access to a bigger customer base are a few of the other benefits of such an alliance, resulting in the opportunity for stronger and better customer service. According to Jianyu et al. (2018), "a strategic alliance is a multifaceted relationship among companies that seek sharing for business development purposes".

The authors pointed out that we often think that only the non-competitive business enterprises could engage in a strategic alliance. However, as a businessperson, it is not only beneficial, but also healthy to engage into strategic alliance with both the competitive and non-competitive firms. The major aspect of strategic alliance is considered to be honesty, integrity and the consideration that the alliance is vital for the growth and success of the business.

7.2 Establishing a Strategic Alliance

Strategic alliance presents a platform in which the members can share their resources, establish strong management expertise, as well as enhance their competitive positions. However, it is critical for a business to evaluate the partners before entering into a strategic alliance. Below is a check-list that you can apply before entering into a strategic alliance:

- Similarity of the long-term and short-term objectives, goals and ambitions
- Similarity of the organization cultures and styles of management and leadership
- Similarities of the business positions and adopted philosophies
- Compatibility of the business assets, skills sets, weaknesses and efficiencies
- Deployment of the strategies that fit
- The compatibility of the financial situations
- Existence of a synergy among aspects of services, products and markets
- The respect and willingness to honor others reputation and business image

Relying on a self-contained strategy of a new unknown market could waste precious time, money and involve costly research and staff effort with an end result that could in fact be detrimental to your company and its reputation or be a total failure. Another drawback of new market development could also be product obsolescence by the time the product is brought into the market. Strategic alliances are basically cooperative agreements between potential or actual competitors. They can be formal ventures for a long term with equity positions or the can be short term agreements, where two or more companies cooperate on a specific task for a specified period of time. While competitors' collaboration may be attractive in some circumstances, even fashionable by today's standards, it has its positive and negative points. You may collaborate with your competitors, either actual or potential, for various strategic purposes (Ohmae, 1989; Kale et al., 2000).

7.3 Advantages of Strategic Alliance

There are four major advantages of strategic alliances:

1. Strategic alliances may help you to enter into a foreign market more quickly than you could have done on your own. Having a local partner can help you better understand business conditions, environments and give you immediate access to good business connections.
2. The cost of developing and establishing a new product or offering a new service or process can be shared through alliance. This may help you manage your bottom line with a proportional investment rather than subject your company to total development costs and the potential risk of new product/ service failure.
3. Strategic alliances can also bring you together with companies that provide skills and assets not currently offered by or available to your company. This saves you time and money in the development cost of those skills and prevents a drain on company assets.
4. Alliances can give your company's product or service credibility in the marketplace by affiliating with a known industry leader and thereby establishing that product or service as an industry standard.

7.4 Disadvantages of Strategic Alliance

While strategic alliances can be many ways as noted above, there are some disadvantages to take note of:

1. Sharing your new knowledge with a competitor could lead to giving your competitor access to a new, low cost way to enter a market and accumulate technology in products or service that you have spent valuable resources on to develop (Kale, 2000).
2. Alliances can cost your company of its developing and processing skills that are the basis for your competitive success. While short term profits may be attractive, the long term result is to leave you with little or no competitive advantage in the global marketplace. Your competitor may be protecting high-paying jobs and value-added positions, while taking valuable development and technology out of your company leaving you with little more than a shell of what you were before.

7.5 The Power of Partnerships

It is inevitable that "Businesses Are Better and Stronger Together".

Strategic partnerships are vital in improving business outcomes. While some business owners believe that the success of a business is a function of their business strategy and competitive advantage, most businesses are currently embracing the idea of partnerships to reduce increased competition for the same customers and collaborate to stay stronger together (Clinton et al., 2016). Business entities engaging in partnerships often broaden their relevance in the markets and increase strengths.

Businesses opting to work together benefit from the strengths and offering each organization brings to the table that extends to the businesses themselves, employees, and the customers. There are various ways in which your organization can stay stronger in partnership by helping grow your business.

7.5.1 Access to New Customers

Strategic partnerships involve both parties sharing their strengths to enable them to grow together. Getting into a strategic partnership has the benefit of extending your business' reach to a wider variety of customers than previously explored. For example, a strategic partnership between a local coffee shop and a book store will help both businesses reach for new customers who enjoy both their products. A book store can even accommodate a small coffee kiosk in its business, and the coffee shop develops a small book section in its business, thereby growing their business stronger together.

7.5.2 Building Brand Trust

Getting into partnerships helps businesses grow in many ways, including increased attention to your business brand. Often, brand trust is achieved through successful business partnerships. The challenge, therefore, involves choosing the right partner during partnership development. The outcomes of your business partnership have an effect on your business brand. According to Arslan (2018), individuals observing your business partnership working well will be interested in ways of generating profits out of similar partnerships and consequently building your brand trust.

7.5.3 Developing New Perspectives

Strategic partnerships in business can be described as "symbiotic" agreements where each partner is set to benefit from the other. A business engaged in strategic partnerships is likely to grow stronger together, exploring new perspectives to their businesses by learning from each other. As a business owner, you may have blind spots, while conducting your business alone; however, a strategic partnership may bring a new perspective that may help in spotting what your business may have missed leading to increased growth.

7.5.4 Increased Moral Support

Operating business entities can be challenging, and you may need moral support whenever you encounter setbacks. Choosing the right partner may offer the opportunity to brainstorm, develop new ideas and cope with any business frustrations necessary for rejuvenation and increasing productivity (Al-Tabbaa et al., 2019). Operating as a single entity can be frustrating during tough business challenge encounters; a trusted partner will increase the value of the business by acting as a business companion, thus accelerating growth together.

7.6 Types of Strategic Alliances

Business partnerships and alliances are fundamental to business growth; however, it is not all business strategies that lead to business success. Strategic alliances help the agreeing businesses to improve their core business strategies and increase their competitive advantages. Such alliance also helps the partnering companies to achieve increased growth better than they could have achieved on their own. Choosing the right type of alliance, therefore, is key to your business success. There are various types of business alliances that you can form in a bid to increase your business growth.

7.6.1 Pro-competitive Alliance

The pro-competitive alliance involves businesses working together without merging their capitals. Some of the pro-competitive alliances in business involve distribution and manufacturing businesses. As a business owner, forming this alliance will benefit your business from minimal interaction in the business operations and low conflicts (Eunni et al., 2006). A pro-competitive alliance takes advantage of vertical integration, and forming such an alliance will benefit your business by creating value through improved operations. An example of the pro-competitive strategic alliance includes the collaboration between DuPont and Sony in the development of optical memory storage products.

7.6.2 Competitive Strategic Alliance

Often businesses operating in the same industry get into a competitive alliance to establish new markets. The competitive strategic alliance in business is characterized by high interaction levels with high possibilities of conflict. Huda et al. (2019), notes that forming a competitive alliance with business in the same industry would benefit your business through maintenance of your competitive advantage by abating entry of new competitors into the business industry. For example, the competitive alliance between Sony and Panasonic to produce new generation TVs was aimed at changing the competitive environment to prevent another player from entering the business operation line.

7.6.3 Non-competitive Strategic Alliance

The non-competitive alliance is another strategic collaboration that your business in order to achieve success. The non-competitive strategic alliance in business involves collaborative operations between businesses that are distinct from each other. Forming a non-competitive strategic alliance for your business will be characterized by high interactions between your businesses and record low levels of conflicts. Non-competitive alliances are suitable for businesses in the same industry but do not consider themselves direct competitors. For example, a non-competitive alliance exists between General Motors and Isuzu to develop low-cost cars. The two businesses do not consider their alliance competitive.

7.7 Making It Work

Like any other business, business partnerships experience challenges that may hinder their growth. Thus, making business partnerships work requires you to choose the right partners with common business vision and strategic direction (Gompers & Lerner, 1996). As a business owner dreaming of creating a successful business partnership, there are various aspects that you need to take into consideration.

7.7.1 Picking a Partner

Choosing the right business partner may be the difference between your business' success and failure. A good business partner should bring the skills and experience that will support your own in achieving business success. For instance, a prospective partner needs to:

(i) *Have Shared Vision*

While forming a strategic alliance for your business, there is a need to pick a business partner that shares your vision for the business venture. Running a collaborative business will involve communication between the involved parties and decision-making activities. Having a partner with a shared vision will make it easy for your business to demonstrate effective communication processes. Business success depends on the operations towards the business' strategic vision and mission. It will thus, be easier for you and your partner to reach the set goals when working towards the same vision.

(ii) *Skills and Experience to Achieve Set Goals*

Business goals play an important role in helping the focus of the operations towards the desired outcomes. Picking the right partner during a strategic alliance should consider the required skills and experiences that will achieve the set goals. Indeed, a single business may not possess all the skill set and experience required to run the business. While picking the partner, you need to consider the skill set and experiences of the prospective business partner's employees and how they will help you achieve your goals.

(iii) *Respect Fair Play*

- Fair play is a code of conduct in business and ethics. Fairness in business involves treating people with dignity and respect in the business operations.
- Picking a partner who respects fair play in your business would require trust. The right partner, therefore, would be the one you can trust and would be able to fulfill their roles in the partnership arrangements.
- The other criteria to consider while picking the right partner for the business involves legally getting information on the potential partner. Information regarding the potential partner will describe the character traits of the individuals. This is necessary to avoid future conflicts in the alliance.
- Information on the potential partner can also be obtained from former partners, the financial community, and former employees. Also, having a face-to-face meeting is necessary to personally understand the potential partner's vision and goals before getting into a partnership.

7.7.2 Structuring the Agreement

After satisfactorily picking the right partner, you need to move to the next step of structuring the agreement. Partnership agreements need to be equitable, efficient, and mutually beneficial. Often, a business partnership can be hard to sustain; thus, to ensure the safeguard of your business in case of fallout, you ensure the safeguarding of critical business procedures, including product development processes and trade secrets (Gompers & Lerner, 1996).

There are various business partnerships, and in a competitive alliance, there is a need to write your business safeguards into an agreement to avoid future misunderstanding in case of competition. One of the important aspects of strategic alliances is honesty. Getting into a partnership means you stand to mutually benefit from each other. Thus, agreeing to freely share product knowledge and skills should be included in the structuring of the partnership agreement. Similarly, partnership contributions are another important aspect that you should clearly include while structuring your partnership agreements (Gompers & Lerner, 1996).

Partners' contributions in businesses vary, and may include time, resources, and capital. It is important that you clearly outline in the agreement the terms of anticipated contributions. Getting acceptable commitment in advance will help promote trust with your potential partners.

7.7.3 Managing the Deal

Effective Management of a business partnership leads to successful business outcomes. A good partnership can scale up your business to new unprecedented heights. Once you have entered into a strategic partnership agreement, paying attention to the cultural differences and effective Management of the resulting management styles is vital in ensuring better partnership relationships (Kale et al., 2000). Managing cultural differences may include ensuring effective communication in your business to increase accountability and encourage increased communication of new ideas and approaches from both businesses. Effective communication would build strong interpersonal relationships between the two businesses leading to success.

Learning from your alliance is another effective way of managing a successful partnership deal. Businesses have different capabilities; thus, learning the strengths and weaknesses of your partners will help in focusing on how the partnership will work together to achieve the common goals of the business. For instance, if your business has a partner better in sales and another in closing sales, then determining how to work differently with your partners to achieve success would be a vital step.

Similarly, the purpose of forming a business alliance is to achieve the level of success that you could not achieve on your own. Thus, better management of the partnership deal would involve to learning from your partners and applying the knowledge in your own business for better outcomes.

7.8 Negotiation Styles and Strategies in Thailand

The negotiation styles and strategies in Thailand is tied to their cultural and historical background. As the only country in Southeast Asia to never have been colonized by foreign powers, Thai consider themselves authentically free, and this freedom is made evident in just about every form of activity you find ethnic Thais including business negotiations. Thailand has a population comprising of about 80% ethnic Thai and a minority dominated by Chinese. Among business owners, many are from the Chinese minority, and most times with ties back in China, making it quite common to find businesses being negotiated on multiple fronts; in Thailand and China or wherever the business owner has strong family connection which can impact business decisions. Statistics indicate that 95% of the Thai population is Buddhists and a majority of the remaining 5% is Muslims. The history of Thailand shows that what we have today has its origins in two former kingdoms; Thai Lann in the North of the country and

7.8 Negotiation Styles and Strategies in Thailand 63

Siam in the South, the division of power among the political elite still follow this structure, and business negotiations often times find themselves also negotiating on these two fronts negotiating separate deals.

7.8.1 Cultural Considerations During Negotiations

Business owners and government officials notably those outside of Bangkok have limited exposure to other cultures, this can lead a situation of people expecting that things should be done according to their way, the culture they grew up with, and has been associated with those that were in the same business before them. There are, however, variations when dealing with businesspeople or officials who are exposed to cultures beyond Thailand or younger people who are more open to doing things in different ways because they have been exposed to other cultures either from traveling or the ubiquitous features of the internet which brings people in contact with other cultures. You can literally Google any business in any part of the world, or watch YouTube videos of different negotiation styles and practices. Those who have experienced other cultures either in person or through the internet would be more amenable to inculcating foreign ideas into their business and negotiation styles.

Culturally, Thais are group-oriented with little room for individualism. They consider conformity to the group as a way of maintaining harmony within the group which can strengthen bonds within the collective, because trust is essential in Thai culture and is paramount before concluding any business negotiations. Thai people will hardly enter into negotiations with people they do not trust even if it costs them the business connection. Thus, trust creates knowledge and awareness of the values of the potential business relation, Thais will only do business with people they know, who value and respect their culture. The relationship usually extends beyond the business; business associates are considered family in a sense. This perspective exposes an interesting take, when the business is between two businesses, it is important for Thai people that the business contacts remain relatively unchanged, in as much as the business is between two business entities, what drives it is the trust between the touchpoints of the organizations. Drastic changes in touchpoint personnel tend to have an effect on the business because it has taken time to gain the trust of an individual, starting afresh with a new teal leading negotiation requires time and effort as the bonding and trust building process will be repeated, and until the people involved are comfortable with the new personnel, the relationship may hinder continued business between the two firms.

Respect is equally important in business perception in Thailand. The respect accorded an individual depends mostly on the age and rank of the individual within the organization. You are expected to introduce yourself and greet older people first, with hands being held together in the form of praying when greeting your negotiating counterparts. According less respect than normal can lead to reputational damage. Hence, it is quite difficult for Thais to engage in business with people whose age or rank within an organization is unclear. To avoid reputational damage, Thai people regard "saving face" acts as essential for maintaining concord in the relationship. Emotional outbursts are strongly discouraged; partners are expected to exhibit maturity that avoids creating embarrassing situations for others during negotiations. Openly criticizing someone especially someone older or higher in rank within an organization can create irreparable discord capable of leading to a breakdown of negotiations because someone has been caused to "lose face" by the actions or comments of another. Thais are naturally friendly and regarded as people who are always smiling not minding the situation, they see life as something to be appreciated and enjoyed with a positive attitude, which they expect business associates to exude during negotiations.

Ethnic Thais prefer being addressed in the order of their names, which is first name and then last name, adding Khun or Phee before the first name is acceptable within the Thai culture. Using Mr. or Ms. Before the first name may cause some confusion especially to Thais with little or no exposure to cultures beyond Thailand. For Thais with Chinese ethnic background, they will prefer being addressed with their surname first as is done in Chinese culture. Where the first name is made up of two names, the generational name is mostly preferred. The two names are mostly hyphenated but usually spoken and written as one. Other Thai people adopt a foreign first name for convenience, when this happens; they usually introduce themselves with their westernized name first followed by their family name. Professional and academic titles must be used where concerned because Thais place a high value on such titles.

After the greeting and introduction pleasantries, offer your business card to all that are present using your right hand, not having one or enough for everyone present is considered unprofessional even though they may not reciprocate the gesture. In case they reciprocate, always accept using the right hand, with a smile, and examine the card with care. Thais may interpret not reading their business cards as an insult. Also, never put it in the back pocket or write on the car in their presence, this is considered disrespectful. The business cards are expected to be of high quality, printed in English and the reverse side translated in Thai. Your business card should state your professional and academic titles where applicable. Small talks are allowed for the negotiators to gauge the mood of the others and acquaint themselves with each other; it is advised to allow the local party to decide the direction of the small talk so as not to cross cultural boundaries concerning topics that are permitted for discussion in public spaces. If this is the first meeting, the main goal really is to become acquainted with each and build trust between the negotiating entities. Show some patience and do not expect very decision to be solved during the first meeting. Make your presentations and material lucid and self-explanatory, it is advantageous to include Thai translations of English documents, it connotes someone who is very professional and helps in accentuating the content of communication.

7.8.2 Negotiation Styles

Understanding your position in business negotiations is fundamental. In Thailand, negotiations are considered as meetings to come to an agreement over mutually beneficial ventures. The positions they occupy depend on the commodity on offer, but mostly, the buyer is considered superior, but it behooves on the negotiating parties to come to a binding agreement that satisfies all the parties involved. In committing to agreements, the business entities hope to agree to long-term agreements with beneficial terms for those involved. Thais naturally negotiate using a cooperative approach, where both parties should be open to some form of compromise in order to advance the negotiation, best described as a win–win situation. When negotiating with Thais from a Chinese background, the style of negotiation might also change to take into account some Chinese cultural influences. Thais rarely disclose information about business during negotiations because they consider as giving up part of the trade secrets which would put them in a position weakness, nonetheless, sharing information during negotiation can increase the level of trust between the negotiating parties.

Negotiations are also expected to be slow and prolonged as this allows for bonding, trust building and relationship formation between the parties involved. Thais are less conscious of time compared to Europeans or North Americans who expect agreements to be reached as soon as agreeable. Settling deadlines or "take it or leave it" offers may be ineffectual in these circumstances, the key word is patience and perseverance until an agreement is reached. Katz (2017) describes this as the polychronic style of work; pursuing multiple actions and goals at the same time. They look at the issues as a whole, jumping from one topic to another in haphazard manner. It is important to keep your eyes on the ball during this non-sequential order of addressing sticky points of negotiations, do not show irritation, instead, relax and try to understand the disposition of your counterpart. Instead, you can try to refocus by emphasizing on already secured agreements. If they continue stalling on trivial issues, then it is most likely there may be an issue they are not willing to share or it might also be a negotiation tactic to obtain more concession. When in doubt, ask open questions politely to find out what might cause hesitation on the part of your negotiating counterpart. Also remember that Thai people love bargaining and haggling and see it as an essential part of negotiation to obtain concession with prices moving significantly from the initial positions between 40 and 60% less in some situations.

Thai negotiators avoid assertive and uncompromising stances during negotiations, its is best not to put them under this type of situations to avoid "face saving situation" already discussed earlier. Making them lose face is irreparable and can bring negotiation to a halt. Instead, you can make personal appeals for them to reconsider their stance based on prevalent conditions. Gratification during negotiation is to some extent generic in both the public and private sectors of Thailand. Depending on who is involved, minor payments can be regarded as gratitude for a successful outcome and expectation instead of a bribe. This is a slippery slope as the lines between a bribe and a gift can be become blurred especially for those coming from the western background where every payment is disclosed in company documents, and in most cases, employees are not allowed to accept gifts from firms that conduct business the employee's organization. However, do not make the mistake of expressing your feelings about things you consider unethical based on your own culture, this could also create a face-saving situation where Thai negotiators may have no choice but to terminate negotiations.

Chapter 8
Customer Service—Listen to What They Say

Abstract Chapter eight of this book details the relevance of customer service in running businesses. This is part of the feedback that enables businesses to refocus and review operations by listening to what their customers have to say about their interactions with the brand. Businesses that neglect this very important message usually have short life spans because rivals take advantage of some of these feedbacks as part of opposition research. The chapter runs through some of the important components of feedback mechanism including the process of active listening, how to listen to customers feedback, and ways of improving customer experience based on the feedbacks received. Businesses are enjoined to keep the channels of communication open as feedback is an ongoing process that continues as long as the business operations are ongoing.

8.1 Active Listening to Customers

The success of customer services is the primary goal of every business organization. Having satisfied customers makes the difference between the business' success or failure. Thus, the process of satisfying customers comes down to the understanding of the customer needs from the basic level with each encounter when the individuals make contact with your business (Itani, 2019). Active listening in customer service, thus involves a process of being totally focused on what the customers say and addressing the needs of these customers.

As a business owner, there is a need to understand that customers want to be heard. It is a human experience to express thoughts and feelings regarding particular issues. However, people also have a poor listening ability as they can only process few words per minute compared to the number of thoughts during the same time. Therefore, understanding the customers' needs requires that you try to understand their thoughts and feeling towards your business, products, and services and use them to promote business growth. According to Weger et al. (2014), 60% of the business' problems result from poor communication between the customers and the business owners. Listening to the customer's needs is vital to providing a great customer service experience and, more importantly, increased business growth.

Similarly, active listening plays an essential role in understanding the customer's needs and wants. Active listening helps create a channel where the customers will communicate what they want you to sell to them. Listening to your customers' opinions and feelings can be achieved through listening to customers' opinions online through social media platforms or through gathering feedback surveys regarding your products and services. As a business owner, every customer feedback influences the business in a particular way, and reacting to the customer feedbacks may be a pivot to business success. Addressing the needs of your customers expressed through interaction feedback will make the existing customers to appreciate your business and also attract new customers.

Active listening also fosters empathy and understanding. Often most interaction between the customers involves problems on particular products or services. When a customer contacts your customer service, they expect to have their problems solved, and any failure may lead to loss of customers. There is thus a need for customer service to exhibit patience and calmness while addressing the customers' concerns (Weger et al., 2014). Active listening is thus vital in situations where the customers express frustration and hostility. Trying to understand the customers' concerns, especially through showing empathy and relaying back to the client's situation, makes the customers feel their problems are being addressed and will lead to increased trust.

8.2 How to Listen to Customers

There are various approaches that you can use to actively listen to your customers. These include:

- Focusing on what the customer is saying as opposed to the response you will give. Paying undivided attention can be achieved by putting aside any distracting thoughts.
- Encouraging the customer by showing that you are tracking his or her conversation. The encouragements may include the use of short verbal feedbacks or body language such as nodding.
- Avoiding interruptions while the customer is talking, unless only when you need clarification.
- Focusing your attention on the client by avoiding destructions and creating a calm environment.
- Paraphrasing the statements that the customers make by repeating them in your own words. Paraphrasing help make the customer understand that you are paying attention to what they are saying.
- Avoiding arguments when interacting with the customers. Offering opinions may be negative, especially where the customer is not happy. It is advisable, therefore, to remain silent and only offer opinions when the customer requests.

- Asking guiding questions. Often, rephrasing what the customer has said in your own words will help in staying in the same line with the customer's needs. If you do not understand correctly, the customer will have the chance to clarify.
- Understanding that it is possible to talk much, but it is rarely possible to listen too much. The customers need to be heard, and thus respecting this rule will require you not to be afraid of being silent.

8.3 Importance of Listening to Customers

Understanding the process of actively listening to your customers helps meet their needs and consequently leads to improved business in various ways. As a business owner, you need to improve your listening skills to understand the customer's opinions about your products and how you can improve your products and services (Place, 2019). Thus, the benefits of active listening to customers affect the overall growth of the business. These are discussed below.

8.3.1 Improved Relationship with the Customers

Business organizations cannot exist without customers, thus meeting the client's needs plays a fundamental role in the growth of the business. Often, customers interact with your business with different needs, from purchasing to sorting out their problems. Sorting out the customer needs in case of a problem helps improve the customer relations with your clients and may lead to the creation of customer loyalty (Place, 2019). In business, if you do not treat your customers well, there are other businesses that may treat them better. Solving the customer needs through active listening improves the customer relationships by making them feel that they can depend on you and become loyal. A strong customer value is vital in ensuring business growth.

8.3.2 Creating New Customers

Customers are the best promoters of business through word of mouth. Positive interactions between your business and the customers may lead the regular customers to spread words regarding their experiences from your company, and this will consequently attract new customers, if the words spread are positive. With the advancements in technology and the growth of social media platforms, clients are always talking about their experiences and are more likely to promote their positive experiences on the social media. Gaining new customers can be achieved through joining the online customer conversations and letting them know that you value their opinions. You can join the customer's conversations online by searching for hashtags and or using the relevant tools to notify you when discussions about your business occur online.

8.3.3 Avoiding Crisis

While the business customers play a role in promoting the business, it is not always that your business may get the positive words. Customer interactions with your business may occur in different ways. Prompt action in times of complaints may avert a possible business crisis that may hinder business growth. For instance, customer reviews on your business website and social media page may not always be positive, and a quick reaction may avoid a business crisis (Florea & Duica, 2017). While interacting with your customers online, it is important that you search all social media platforms and respond promptly to any customer frustrations and complaints. Quick response to customers on social media platforms such as Twitter and Facebook helps increase the customers' confidence in your business and the assurance that they can rely on you.

8.4 Keeping the Conversation Going

Active listening to your customers involves the development of deep trust with your clients and the creation of long-term loyalty. Having a clear understanding of your customers' needs also requires keeping an ongoing interaction to achieve a deeper understanding. Meaningful conversations can be achieved through face-to-face conversations; however, with the increased online interaction, they can also be achieved through social media interactions. As a business owner, there are various ways you can use to keep the conversation going to gain a better understanding of the customers' needs. For instance, asking for recommendations. The customer's opinions and feeling about particular products and services play a vital role in understanding their needs (Reed et al., 2016). As a business, keeping the conversation going may include asking questions on opinions and thoughts about products and services to better improve and meet the customer needs. Interacting with your customers online may include asking your followers for recommendations on your business. The responses will offer an insight into your customers' thoughts, preferences, and behaviors.

Similarly, promoting community events can keep the conversation going. Businesses can also keep the conversation with their customers going through attending or hosting community events. Naturally, individuals will tend to be associated with people or businesses they like. Asking your customers if they will attend a local

8.4 Keeping the Conversation Going

football match will keep the interactions going and may lead to meaningful interactions that will make a difference in your business. For instance, sharing stories of communities pulling together will align your business with community needs and will help increase your customer base.

Chapter 9
Implementation, Monitoring and Evaluation—Now What Do We Do?

Abstract This chapter highlights steps to be undertaken once the business operation is up and running. After all the planning, meetings, agreements, and personnel have been put in place, the next stage is to implement all the grand ideas and see how they would run in the field. Once implementation has occurred, the process has to be monitored for compliance and evaluated to find out steps and policies that should be continued, those to be modified and the ones to be halted and a new direction for those that do not go according to plan. Some details to consider during implementation are also discussed such as budgeting and allocation of resources, communication strategies, challenges and benefits of monitoring and evaluation.

9.1 Now What Do We Do?

After developing the various business strategies that can take our business to the next level, the question that arises is: "Now what do we do?" In the previous eight chapters, this book has discussed various aspects and strategies that the businessperson should consider adopting and implementing—global competitiveness, marketing and positioning yourself, innovation, using information and leveraging resources, technology, human resource and cultural communication, strategic alliance and customers services. However, these strategies need to be put into practice in order to benefit the organization. That brings us to the answers to the question posed at the beginning of this paragraph. The answers as to what we should do lie in these three words: implementation, monitoring and evaluation.

> Implementation implies 'the practice of carrying out, execution of a plan, an idea, a model, a specification, or a standards policy for the purpose of achieving a particular set objective" (Grover et al., 2018).

Implementation is the stage where all the planned activities are put into action. Before the implementation of a project, you, along with any other project committee or executives, should identify your product's strengths and weaknesses (internal forces), opportunities and threats (external forces) through a basic SWOT Analysis.

On the other hand, monitoring and evaluation provides information on how the adopted strategies are performing, what the intervention implemented is doing, and whether the targeted goals and objectives are being achieved or not. It also provides a guidance for future intervention activities, as well as it is considered as an important aspect of achieving accountability for funding agencies and stakeholders.

By definition, monitoring refers to the "regular observation, assessment, and collection of information regarding the implemented project or strategy". It is used to demonstrate whether things are going as they were planned, keeps track of the project inputs and outputs, such as activities, reports and documents, financing and budgeting, as well as supplies and equipment. You should consider monitoring activities as an everyday activity.

Evaluation is a business activity, which "seeks to evaluate and find out whether the business is achieving the objectives it was set to achieve" (Pearlson et al., 2019). It assesses the difference before and after implementation of a recommended strategy or idea. It even goes further to determine why the why the observed difference actually occurred.

9.2 Implementation

9.2.1 How to Carry Out a Successful Implementation

Business implementation turns the plans and strategies into action to achieve the set goals and objectives. Conducting business strategy implementation is essential, just like the strategic plans themselves. Having a great business plan will amount to nothing if you do not take action to implement the plan. According to (Candido & Santos, 2015), many businesses fail due to failure to implement their strategic plans. Failure to implement the business' strategic plans is often due to the failure to link the organization's strategic plans to budgeting as well as linking the organization's employee incentives to the strategic plans. Successful implementation of strategic plans involves understanding the implementation process and the stakeholders. As a business owner, you need to address the *who, where, when, and how* to implement the strategic plans. To ensure the successful implementation of your company's business plan, you need to follow various steps in the process.

9.2.2 Communication of the Strategic Business Plan

Although the strategies are communicated during the strategy formulation, it is also important to communicate the plan before you implementation. The communication should address issues with respect to initiatives, budgets, and expected performance. In this first step of implementation, you need to clarify your business goals and strategies to all members involved and the strategies that will be used to achieve the set plans (Ramsing, 2009). Communicating the business plan and the strategies to be

9.2 Implementation 75

used in implementing the plans has the effect of boosting employees' morale. As a business owner, you need to review the outcomes and performances of the strategic business plan to determine the possible success and failures. Past experiences should be used to communicate what success should look like.

9.2.3 Developing the Implementation Structure

The next step in ensuring the successful implementation of your business strategy will involve the creation of the structure that will guide the implementation. The implementation structure process requires that you build out a road map for achieving the strategy expectations of your team to eliminate implementation confusion. Essentially, you need to determine the roles and responsibilities to be performed by your team in implementing the strategic plan as well as the skills required to have the tasks done. In this phase also, there is a need for you to establish the coordination mechanisms between the teams involved in the implementation of the strategic plan. The establishment of the coordination mechanisms will help facilitate the delegation of duties and responsibilities among the teams.

9.2.4 Developing Implementation Support Policies and Programs

Developing the implementation support policies aims at encouraging and aiding the strategy implementation process. As a project manager, some of the support programs you may establish will include the performance tracking systems to evaluate the progress of the implementation strategies. Also, it is vital to establish performance management systems to encourage the teams working on the projects. For instance, the performance management systems should be developed to encourage employee involvement Ensuring successful implementation of your business strategy will therefore require the establishment of support programs to evaluate progress through daily, weekly, and monthly reports.

9.2.5 Budget and Resource Allocation

Allocating resources towards the implementation of the business strategies is one of the most important steps towards successful implementation. It enables the teams to perform their tasks and functions well. In implementing your business plans, therefore, you need to allocate resources to the departments involved based on the budgetary requirements from each department, and also maintain checks and balances to ensures all teams are working within budgetary limits.

9.2.6 Discharging Implementation Activities

After performing the implementation planning and allocating budgetary resources, the last step to successful business implementation would include putting the strategies and tactics into action. Discharging of the implementation tactics and action would require the participation of your organization's leadership. As a leader in your business, there are various leadership styles you can employ to ensure better implementation of the business strategies. For instance, engaging with the employees in implementing the projects will help in understanding their strengths and weaknesses and, where necessary, provide training for successful project implementation. Similarly, at this level, it is important to enforce control measures in the performance of the tasks.

9.2.7 Avoiding Business Implementation Pitfalls

Every business needs a strategic plan and hopes for the successful implementation of these plans. However, in some cases, the implementation of the business strategies does not always turn out successful. According to Kaplan (2005), 90% of business organizations fail in the effective implementation of their strategic plans. As a project manager, there is a need to understand the common challenges that could lead to business implementation failures and how to avoid them to ensure success in your project implementations. Acknowledging the common challenges in strategy implementation is essential in ensuring successful business implementation strategies. There are various reasons that lead to business implementation failures. Some of those reasons are discussed below.

9.2.8 Weak Strategy

A strong strategy is a roadmap to effective business plan implementation. Having a weak strategy will lead to unclear timelines and poor objectives which will likely to lead to failure. Often, poor strategy objectives are as a result of not investing enough time in setting up the strategy. As a project manager, drafting up a strong strategy should be a priority to ensure strategy success. For example, you need to focus on the business objectives instead of trying to make everyone happy through vague objectives. Also, setting up strong business strategy objectives can be achieved through the use of the SMART concept which involves the setting up of specific, measurable, achievable, realistic and timely results of the objectives.

9.2.9 Ineffective Staff Training

Business employees play an important role in the implementation of the set business strategies. For a strategy to get off the ground, the employees are expected to effectively execute set roles and responsibilities to ensure success. However, lack of proper employee training may be a recipe for sluggish strategy implementation that may lead to failure (Ivančić, 2013). As a project manager, understanding the need for proper business learning for the employees is vital just as having skilled staff for effective implementation. You can avoid the challenge of ineffective employee output by providing the right training and learning opportunities among the staff and following up to ensure that the workers employ the learned skills in their daily workflows.

9.2.10 Poor Communication

Communication plays an important role in various business operations. In the implementation of business strategies, communication is vital in the execution of the plans and should be initiated from the top-down. Poor communication leads to poor coordination between project teams and leads to widespread uncertainty in the business strategy. As a project manager, you can avoid the challenge of poor communication during the execution of business strategies through the practice of transparent and honest communications concerning the implementation of the business strategy. A clear understanding of the possible strengths and weaknesses in the project plans will motivate the employees to ensure implementation success.

9.2.11 Poor Follow Through

Execution of new business strategies needs to be evaluated from time to time. Poor implementation follow-through, therefore, occurs when the project managers fail to routinely review the execution activities. Executing business strategies involves the incorporation of various departments and teams to get things done. Thus, getting off track can be easy with little distractions, and this will lead to implementation failure. While managing your strategic implementation processes, you can avoid the challenges of poor follow-through by holding regular reviews to determine the progress of the implementation processes. The availability of big data is a resource firms should actively explore towards scaling up to maximize business potentials (Chaveesuk et al., 2020).

9.3 Monitoring and Evaluation

As outlined in the implementation process, business strategies are a process, and successful implementation requires continuous review to determine performance progress. Monitoring and evaluation (M&E) thus are processes that enable the review, analysis, and understanding of strategic plan performance during implementation (Dos Santos, 2014). The aim of conducting the monitoring and evaluation process on business strategies is to ensure the improvement of the current and future management of the project's outputs and outcomes. As a project manager, you need to develop a monitoring and evaluation plan at the beginning of every strategic business program to ensure a clear program is in place to monitor and evaluate the progress and ensures the success of the plans.

9.3.1 Developing Monitoring and Evaluation Strategy

Developing an Effective monitoring and evaluation strategy set the framework for the correct and accurate improvement of the business strategies. Project managers need to conduct research before developing effective monitoring and evaluation strategies. Some of the steps in the development of the M&E strategies are discussed below:

9.3.2 Defining Measurable Benchmarks

The business projects' progress can only be evaluated based on set targets. Thus, while designing an effective monitoring and evaluation program, you need to define the requirements and targets that the actual project results are going to be compared against (Crawford & Bryce, 2003). Setting benchmarks for evaluation can be achieved through the use of the historical data prior to the implementation of the project or conducting a consultation process to determine how the project is expected to impact the business stakeholders.

9.3.3 Communicating Benchmarks

The monitoring and evaluation strategies involve various stakeholders, including the employees. Effective monitoring and evaluation processes serve as the quality controls to the business's strategic plans. Communicating the benchmarks to your employees is thus vital for them to understand the quality controls that will be used in evaluating the strategic business plans (Crawford, 2003). As a project manager, however, you need to take into consideration the validity of the benchmarks. Effective monitoring and evaluation benchmarks should take into account the current industry performance to ensure the relevance of the program.

9.3.4 Developing Monitoring Plans

The monitoring plans form the basis of the monitoring and evaluation strategies. Every strategic business project requires different monitoring and evaluation style. However, there are specific monitoring requirements that every strategy should be based on. Some of the monitoring requirements you should consider while developing the M&E plans should include reporting requirements needed for communication. Also, the strategy will need quality requirements to be used as a basis for evaluating the business strategies. The other requirements will include the business requirements, risk, and client needs.

9.3.5 Establishment of the Review Plans

A review of the monitoring and evaluation plans offers an analysis of the actual performance against the set benchmarks. In establishing the review plans, you may need to conduct evaluation reviews after every project under the strategic business plan. At this stage, you need to consider issues such as how the M&E processes will be communicated to the employees (Crawford, 2003). Also, during the establishment of the reviews, there is a need to determine how the evaluation processes can be used by the workers to ensure the efficiency of the strategic business plans. As a project manager, you need to understand that reviewing involves the analysis of the reasons that may lead to deviations from the set benchmarks of the strategic business plans. And once the strategy is developed, it needs to be implemented to achieve the desired results.

9.4 Benefits of Monitoring and Evaluation in Business Strategies

The development of monitoring and evaluation programs for strategic business plans plays an important role in offering management insights, including resource allocation, business growth, and future business projections. Often, the development of the M&E process takes into account the historical data on similar business strategies (Zwikael, 2018). The historical data can be retrieved from previous monitoring and evaluation reports and can be used by the project managers to determine the growth and progress of the business.

Also, the development of the monitoring and evaluation strategies is vital in identifying possible problems in the strategic business plans and helps the management to address them before they can escalate (Zwikael, 2018). Monitoring and evaluation reports are done at the end of every business project. The routine reporting makes it easy to detect any strategic plan anomaly or problem and makes it easier to solve problems so detected compared to the annual reporting of the business strategies progress.

Similarly, developing monitoring and evaluation strategies is important in highlighting possible opportunities to the business projects that may help the business to grow. Development of the strategic business plans forms the benchmarks that the business process needs to achieve; however, effective strategies may lead to other opportunities that may ensure expanded business growth. For instance, routine monitoring and evaluation can highlight the business process that worked well and can be used in future strategies to ensure growth.

9.5 Challenges of Monitoring and Evaluation Process

While the incorporation of the monitoring and evaluation processes in strategic business plans leads to unprecedented success, there are various challenges that affect the effective implementation of the processes. For instance, many organizations try to minimize costs while maximizing their profits; thus, incorporating monitoring and evaluation programs on the business' strategic plans may be considered costly (Dos Santos, 2014). Limited financial and staff resources thus come out as a challenge in the establishment of effective business and monitoring programs.

Similarly, the establishment of effective M&E processes may be challenged by gaps in knowledge and experience in the definition of the performance indicators. The establishment of business projects monitoring and evaluation processes is continuous, and every new project requires specific performance indicators. Many organizations thus are challenged by lack of experience from their staff requiring new training programs, which may be costly to the business organizations. Lastly, the project timelines also constitute challenges to the effective establishment of monitoring and evaluation programs. Large organizations have multiple strategic programs that may take years to develop effective monitoring and evaluation systems. Thus, racing against time to develop effective M&E programs for the various business strategic programs can be challenging.

Chapter 10
Social Responsibility—Giving Something Back

Abstract The final chapter dwells on social responsibility and how firms should always have a program dedicated to social responsibility functions. The sole focus of business entities should not only be profit, but also societal good and how to help individuals and organizations whose goals align with that of the firm and contribute to a better society. These could be community groups, rights groups, student groups, or some other social justice non-governmental organization. The chapter details ways of giving back and how to get employees involved, and recommends what part of the profit to invest in social responsibility. Benefits of social responsibility are outlined and strategies to be deployed. The firm should consider itself as part of the community by contributing to causes and developments that benefit the society.

10.1 Giving Something Back

No matter how big or small your business is, there is one thing that is quite hard to ignore, the business environment and society in which the business is carried out. It is important and equally beneficial for business owners to retrospect and ask, "How should we give back to the society?" This brings in the concept of social responsibility. By definition, social responsibility implies the business practice that involves participating in the initiatives that benefits the society. It is also referred to as the social conscience or social citizenship. They include the initiatives that are run by the businesses in order to evaluate and take the responsibility of the impact they have caused to the society, covering the issues, which range from environment to the human rights.

Social responsibility is a self-regulatory mechanism, which is usually included in the business plan, with an objective of focusing on achieving the economic, social and environmental benefits for all the stakeholders involved, including: employees, consumers, investors, suppliers, customers as well as the society at large. Environmental scanning must also be utilized to identify factors that could affect marketing success. This process is especially important in determining opportunities and threats. Today, the Internet is probably the most important global and technological change in the determining product environment. Customer databases are more readily available to companies so that products and services can be developed to more closely match those customers' needs. Environmental scanning can also help you monitor and maintain social trends and the ability to maintain close relationships with your customers in areas such as growth or shifts in population as well as monitor competitive and economic environments. There are various ways in which a business could give back to the society. These include:

- Employee education and training
- Social Activity
- Environmental control
- Employee relations, benefits and satisfaction with work
- Safety and health care for employees

A business could also assume responsibility towards:

- Customer
- Employees
- Shareholders
- Communities
- Environment

10.2 Giving Back to Business

Giving back to the society is important in supporting the growth and well-being of the community, as well as keeping the business doors open. It is a means of indirectly supporting the growth of the business. As a business owner, one of the evident and benefits you can derive from the social responsibility is the business promotion. It is a means of promoting the business, which bears beneficial fruits in the long-run (Taylor, 2014). Your contribution activities to the society forever remain at the hearts and minds of those who were both directly and indirectly affected by them. This has a long-run positive image to the business.

Another considerable positive effect of social responsibility is that it generates new business opportunities. Charity activities are a great way of developing business network. When business comes together to carry out a charity work, they create great opportunities for collaborations and development of business partnerships. These create new business opportunities.

10.3 Ways to Give Back to Society

The practice of social responsibility comes with various benefits to the business, including attracting the right talents and building a positive business reputation, and increased consumer appeal to your business, among others. Thus, it is evident that the practice of giving back to society through social responsibility practices plays an important role in business success. With the growing competition in the markets, businesses need to understand the best way to practice giving back to society. As a business owner, there are various ways your company can give back to society and ensure overall business growth.

10.3.1 Getting Your Employees Involved

Employees play an essential role in social responsibility as they are the face of your business. Among the benefits of participating in social responsibility, activities include attracting the right talents to your business. According to Camilleri, (2017), 34% of the millennial workers are motivated to work in organizations involved in community charitable activities. Similarly, a majority of millennial workers are ready to contribute to a company that positively impacts society through social responsibility practices. Thus, getting your employees involved in social responsibilities as a way of giving back to society may involve giving your employees a way to contribute to society. For example, you may involve your employees in volunteer donations towards a positive community activity or choosing a day during a month to encourage and have your employees participate in community activities. Using various options to get your employees involved in community work will make them feel part of a noble cause and will also attract new talents to foster business growth.

10.3.2 Setting Aside Part of the Profits

One way of ensuring your business gives back directly to the community is through the establishment of a scheme that sees part of profits from sales set aside for donation. There are various social activities that a business can get engaged in on a yearly basis, and without proper planning, it may seem a big challenge to achieve the entire all the planned activities. The best way to set aside part of your profits for donations back to society can be in the form of a percentage of your sales. For example, the TOMS shoe business has a scheme that sets aside a percentage from the sale of each shoe towards charitable activities. Setting aside a small percentage of your sales, such as 5% towards charitable community activities, may seem a small amount; however, every little bit towards a charitable cause always goes a long way in ensuring social benefits and resulting in social responsibility benefits.

10.3.3 Being Part of the Community

The other important way of giving back to society as a business is through being part of the community. Often, giving back to the community does not necessarily require offering financial aid, but may include being involved in activities that contribute to the greater benefit of the society. As a business, therefore, you need to determine ways your business may be involved in community causes aimed at the greater benefit of all (Rafique, 2020). For example, if you run a dry-cleaning business, you can engage in community charitable events like cleaning donated clothes for the less fortunate in society for free. Your business can also serve as a collection point for donated clothes to be distributed to the less fortunate, especially coats during the winter season. Being part of the community includes being involved in already existing community events that could use your input and facilities.

10.3.4 Building Communities

Often, many startup businesses hoping to give back to the community may find it hard to offer the financial assistance offered by other established businesses in the market. Thus, to successfully give back to the community, such organizations need to think creatively to benefits from the social responsibility practices. As a start-up business owner, it is important to understand the community that you operate in and the best ways to give back to society. For instance, creating a community aimed at building connections and maintaining a cordial relationship with the community through quarterly fund-raising events will go a long way to build your social community.

10.4 Moral Obligation and Corruption

Based on the concept of social responsibility, every business has a moral duty towards the society in which they operate. Corruption in business involves the misuse of positions of power to gain unfair business advantage. Often corruption activities involve accepting bribes, diversion of business funds, double-dealing, among other activities. Businesses operating in environments with widespread corruption have the moral obligation to take firm stands against corruption. According to Lopatta et al. (2017), stakeholders, including customers and business investors, put a high value on ethical behavior in corrupt environments. Similarly, the international monetary fund estimates corruption to amount to about 2% of the global output.

Resisting corruption in business helps in increasing the competitive advantage and ensuring sustainable growth. There are various ways that businesses can strengthen their practices against corrupt practices. For instance, defining clear roles for the business' top management makes it easier for the business to practice anti-bribery and anti-corruption policies (Crane et al., 2019). Similarly, companies can embed a culture of compliance within their operations. Embedding a culture that values ethics and compliance will involve your business engaging in compliance programs, training, and standard communication regarding compliance to the business' operations.

Widespread corruption often distorts the market competition, while creating cynicism among society members. Businesses can use their social responsibilities to combat the increasing nature of corruption activities in business through the institution of anti-corruption and anti-bribery policies. While many businesses have put in place anti-corruption policies, the implementation of these policies makes a difference in combating corruption. In a business firm, you have the moral obligation to make sure the business staff understands the rules and expectations surrounding bribery and corruption.

10.5 Benefits of Giving Back to the Society

Business activities involving giving back to society are often done without expectations of direct financial rewards; however, social responsibility activities are certainly not without rewards. Many business owners that engaged in charitable social practices derive satisfaction from the pleasant feelings of connectedness and being part of the greater good of the community. Even so, businesses engaged in giving back to the community experience various intangible benefits responsible for fostering business growth and ultimately overall business success. There are various ways in which your business can benefit from giving back to society.

10.5.1 Improved Business Reputation

Participating in charitable business activities aimed at supporting the local communities in which your business operates helps in creating a good relationship with the customers. As a business operating in a particular community environment, it is easier to identify the local needs that your business may target its efforts to give back to society (Verčič & Ćorić, 2018). In return, the community will tend to support your business. Building a good relationship with the community has the benefit of building a strong business reputation that will increase the value of your business. Having a great business reputation is vital in increasing your business' value and ensuring that the community will be able to support you in the future.

10.5.2 Attracting Talent

In the current competitive business markets, having the right workforce determines the chances of success or failure of a business. On the other hand, also, talented workers choose to work with companies that take into account the employee needs and participate in responsible community activities. Thus, the best way to attract talented workers to your company would be through incorporating strategies of giving back to the community. According to Verčič and Ćorić (2018), engaging in activities that make your business a force in community activities has the power to improve your employees regard for the business and helps in retaining talents. Similarly, employees require motivation to improve their productivity, giving back to the community creates a good reputation of your business that will motivate the employees to be part of the greater picture and consequently improve productivity.

10.5.3 Building Connections and Widening Business Networks

In business, valuable connections are an important resource that contributes to business growth. Participating in charitable business activities offers your business the opportunity to establish trust with other players in the industry that may be good business connections in the future. Often, great charitable events and activities are organized by influential individuals in the business industry. Engaging in activities aimed at giving back to the community, therefore, gives your business the opportunity to engage with these individuals and organizations that may become opportunities to expand your business. Improving your community through giving back activities will place you on the path of influential people such as political figures and business moguls. That will go a long way in expanding your business networks and consequently increase growth.

10.6 The Cost of Ignoring Social Responsibility

Social responsibilities in business are moral practices that businesses undertake to ensure a positive influence on society. Some of the activities promoting social responsibility may include minimizing environmental externalities, donating to charity, or promoting volunteerism in businesses. Ignoring social responsibility practices may be highly detrimental to the business. For instance, social responsibility activities promote a better public image for the business. Shunning these activities will paint a negative picture about the business among the consumers and investors due to the unethical reputations, and this may lead to negative effects on your business' competitive advantage (Sprinkle, 2010). Similarly, ignoring business social responsibilities may lead to the risk of reduced employee motivation and lack of self-interest. Poor social responsibility activities may demotivate talents in your company and may lead to struggles in retaining talents. In the current information age, the business' commitment to community plays a great role in influencing the decision of workers to choose particular companies to work for.

10.7 Using Social Responsibility to Build a Sustainable Business

Social responsibility activities are increasingly becoming essential in business today and can be achieved through activities such as reducing carbon footprints, product donations, charity work, employee community service, and environmental policies, among other ways. While socially responsible activities aim to benefit the community, these activities also impact the business operations in the present and future needs. Building business sustainability involves engaging in activities that meet the present business needs without compromising the future ability of the business operations to ensure success. Therefore, as a business owner, implementing the appropriate social responsibility strategies is vital in the creation of a sustainable business.

10.7.1 Building Your Social Responsibility Strategy Around Your Core Competencies

There are various socially responsible activities that businesses can engage in to give back to the community. However, as a business leader, there is a need to determine the most appropriate activity which is in line with your business' core competencies (Ashrafi et al., 2018). Indeed, business social responsibility activities may be viewed by business leaders and risk mitigation activities. Engaging in any socially responsible activity mitigates your business' risk of being viewed as a socially irresponsible venture. However, socially responsible activities can also be opportunities to creating a sustainable business. For instance, a company that has researched and developed strength in the particular business area should build its social responsibilities to support similar causes for the benefits of the community and long-term benefits for the business.

10.7.2 Recognizing the Important Social Issues to Your Customers

Consumers are increasingly interested in business social responsibilities. According to Camilleri (2017), consumers play an important role in business growth and development. Business leaders hoping to develop sustainable businesses take into consideration the needs of their customers both socially and through their preferences. The majority of millennial consumers purchase business products based on the company's social responsibility reputation. Often, consumers reward socially responsible businesses through increasing their brand loyalty and being engaged in the business' charitable activities for the greater good of the community. However, similar consumers can go to extreme extents to punish socially irresponsible businesses through product boycotts and negative business publicity. As a business manager aiming at developing a sustainable business, it is important to recognize social issues that matter to your customers.

10.7.3 Motivating Your Employees

Another way of using social responsibility to build a sustainable business is through development of socially responsible initiatives that motivate your employees. Business managers understand that one of the greatest assets that a business could have are motivated employees. Majority of current workers take into account the levels of business engagements in socially responsible activities. According to Verčič and Verčič (2018), 76% of millennial workers attach great importance to a company's social and environmental commitments. Building a sustainable business would require your business to develop strategies of retaining your productive workforce as well as attracting new talents to ensure improved future business growth. Thus, developing social responsibilities can be used to attract and motivate employees and consequently leading to sustainable growth.

10.8 Bottom Line

The bottom line of every business is to minimize costs while maximizing profits. Building a sustainable business should therefore take into consideration the business' relation of profits. While developing business social responsibility activities, it is important that you take into account how the activities s will affect the business' bottom line (Suganthi, 2020). For instance, in developing socially responsible activities such as engaging in recycling activities to rid the community of pollution, the activities should also be cost-effective for the business to ensure reduced costs and maximization of profits. Often, socially responsible activities can be favorable

10.8 Bottom Line

for the business's bottom line and ensuring sustainable business development. For example, switching to environmentally friendly lighting such as using solar power can be socially responsible while supporting business sustainability.

References

Ackerman, R., & Schibrowsky, J. (2007). A business marketing strategy applied to student retention: A higher education initiative. *Journal of College Student Retention: Research, Theory & Practice, 9*(3), 307–336.

Adel, H. M., Mahrous, A. A., & Hammad, R. (2020). Entrepreneurial marketing strategy, institutional environment, and business performance of SMEs in Egypt. *Journal of Entrepreneurship in Emerging Economies*.

Akter, S., Wamba, S. F., Gunasekaran, A., Dubey, R., & Childe, S. J. (2016). How to improve firm performance using big data analytics capability and business strategy alignment? *International Journal of Production Economics, 182*, 113–131.

Al-Alawi, A. I., Al-Marzooqi, N. Y., & Mohammed, Y. F. (2007). Organizational culture and knowledge sharing: critical success factors. *Journal of knowledge management*.

Al-Sarayrah, S., Tarhini, A., Obeidat, B. Y., Al-Salti, Z., & Kattoua, T. (2016). The effect of culture on strategic human resource management practices: A theoretical perspective. *International Journal of Business Management and Economic Research, 7*(4), 704–716.

Al-Tabbaa, O., Leach, D., & Khan, Z. (2019). Examining alliance management capabilities in cross-sector collaborative partnerships. *Journal of Business Research, 101*, 268–284.

Ariyapruchya, K., Nair, A., Lathapipat, D., Reungsri,T., Mohib, S. S. A., Miralles Murciego, G., Chirwa,S. B. C., Zachau, U., Mishra, D. K., Shetty,S.; Nguyen, H., Vashakmadze, E. T., & De Nicola, F. (2018). Thailand economic monitor: beyond the innovation paradox (English). Washington, D.C.: World Bank Group. http://documents.worldbank.org/curated/en/991791530850604659/Thailand-economic-monitor-beyond-the-innovation-paradox

Arslan, B. (2018). The interplay of competitive and cooperative behavior and differential benefits in alliances. *Strategic Management Journal, 39*(12), 3222–3246.

Ashrafi, M., Adams, M., Walker, T. R., & Magnan, G. (2018). How corporate social responsibility can be integrated into corporate sustainability: A theoretical review of their relationships. *International Journal of Sustainable Development & World Ecology, 25*(8), 672–682.

Autio, E., & Laamanen, T. (1995). Measurement and evaluation of technology transfer: Review of technology transfer mechanisms and indicators. *International Journal of Technology Transfer Management, 10*(6), 643–664.

Azevedo, E. M., & Gottlieb, D. (2017). Perfect competition in markets with adverse selection. *Econometrica, 85*(1), 67–105.

Bertoletti, P., & Etro, F. (2017). Monopolistic competition when income matters. *The Economic Journal, 127*(603), 1217–1243.

Barth, C., & Koch, S. (2019). Critical success factors in ERP upgrade projects. *Industrial Management & Data Systems*.

Belas, J., Strnad, Z., Gavurova, B., & Cepel, M. (2019). Business environment quality factors research—SME management's platform. *Polish Journal of Management Studies, 20*(1), 64–77.

Camilleri, M. A. (2017). Corporate sustainability and responsibility: Creating value for business, society and the environment. *Asian Journal of Sustainability and Social Responsibility, 2*(1), 59–74.

Campbell, C., Sands, S., Ferraro, C., Tsao, H. Y. J., & Mavrommatis, A. (2020). From data to action: How marketers can leverage AI. *Business Horizons, 63*(2), 227–243.

Candido, C., & Santos, S. P. D. (2015). Strategy implementation: What is the failure rate? *Journal of Management & Organization, 21*(02), 237–262.

Carayannis, E. G., Samara, E. T., & Bakouros, Y. L. (2015). *Innovation and entrepreneurship: Theory, policy and practice.* Springer.

Chaveesuk, S., Khalid, B, & Chaiyasoonthorn, W. (2020). Emergence of new business environment with big data and artificial intelligence. In *Proceedings of the 9th International Conference on Information Communication and Management*, August 23–26, 181–185. https://doi.org/10.1145/3357419.3357441

Chaveesuk, S., Khalid, B, & Chaiyasoonthorn, W. (2020). Understanding stakeholder's needs for using blockchain based smart contracts in construction industry of Thailand: Extended TAM framework. Paper presented at the 13th International Conference on Human System Interaction (HSI), 6–8 June, pp. 137–141. https://doi.org/10.1109/HSI49210.2020.9142675

Chung, W. (2001). Identifying technology transfer in foreign direct investment: Influence of industry conditions and investing firm motives. *Journal of International Business Studies, 32*(2), 211–229. https://doi.org/10.1057/palgrave.jibs.8490949

Ciriello, R. F., Richter, A., & Schwabe, G. (2016). Designing an idea screening framework for employee-driven innovation. In *2016 49th Hawaii International Conference on System Sciences (HICSS)*, pp. 4262–4271.

Clinton, H. R., Kaine, T., & Kaine, T. M. (2016). *Stronger together*. Simon and Schuster.

Côrte-Real, N., Ruivo, P., & Oliveira, T. (2020). Leveraging internet of things and big data analytics initiatives in European and American firms: Is data quality a way to extract business value? *Information & Management, 57*(1), 103141.

Cramer, J., & Krueger, A. B. (2016). Disruptive change in the taxi business: The case of Uber. *American Economic Review, 106*(5), 177–182. https://doi.org/10.1257/aer.p20161002

Crane, A., Matten, D., Glozer, S., & Spence, L. (2019). *Business ethics: Managing corporate citizenship and sustainability in the age of globalization.* Oxford University Press.

Crawford, P., & Bryce, P. (2003). Project monitoring and evaluation: A method for enhancing the efficiency and effectiveness of aid project implementation. *International Journal of Project Management, 21*(5), 363–373.

Cristea, A. (2014). Positioning strategies for obtaining and sustaining competitive advantage. *International Journal of Economic Practices and Theories, 4*(5), 894–902.

Crowley, F., & Jordan, D. (2017). Does more competition increase business-level innovation? Evidence from domestically focused firms in emerging economies. *Economics of Innovation and New Technology, 26*(5), 477–488.

Das, S. (1987). Externalities and technology transfer through multinational corporations. *Journal of International Economics, 22*, 171–182. https://doi.org/10.1016/0022-1996(87)90028-6

Dhingra, S., & Morrow, J. (2019). Monopolistic competition and optimum product diversity under firm heterogeneity. *Journal of Political Economy, 127*(1), 196–232.

Dos Santos, M. A. (2014). Implementation, monitoring and evaluation of sustainable business practices: framework and empirical illustration. *Corporate Governance.*

Du Toit, F. (2019). Determine your needs before implementing technology: feature-technology. *Money Marketing, 2019*(Oct 2019), 20–20.

Eunni, R. V., Kasuganti, R. R., & Kos, A. J. (2006). Knowledge management processes in international business alliances: A review of empirical research, 1990–2003. *International Journal of Management, 23*(1), 34.

References

Feldman, D. (2019, July 28). How Netflix is changing the future of movie theaters. *Forbes*. Retrieved from https://www.forbes.com/sites/danafeldman/2019/07/28/how-netflix-is-changing-the-future-of-movie-theaters/?sh=77b4a0af5f46

Florea, N. V., & Duica, A. (2017). Improving communication and relationship with customers using models to measure their value. *Valahian Journal of Economic Studies, 8*(1), 47–56.

Frankenberger, K., Weiblen, T., Csik, M., & Gassmann, O. (2013). The 4I-framework of business model innovation: A structured view on process phases and challenges. *International Journal of Product Development, 18*(3–4), 249–273.

Geissdoerfer, M., Savaget, P., & Evans, S. (2017). The Cambridge business model innovation process. *Procedia Manufacturing, 8*, 262–269.

Ghobakhloo, M. (2020). Determinants of information and digital technology implementation for smart manufacturing. *International Journal of Production Research, 58*(8), 2384–2405.

Gibson, D. V., & Smilor, W. (1991). Key variables in technology transfer: a field—Study based on empirical analysis. *Journal of Engineering and Technology Management, 8*, 287–312. https://doi.org/10.1016/0923-4748(91)90015-J

Gochhayat, J., Giri, V. N., & Suar, D. (2017). Influence of organizational culture on organizational effectiveness: The mediating role of organizational communication. *Global Business Review, 18*(3), 691–702.

Groß, M. (2015). Exploring the acceptance of technology for mobile shopping: An empirical investigation among Smartphone users. *The International Review of Retail, Distribution and Consumer Research, 25*(3), 215–235.

Gompers, P., & Lerner, J. (1996). The use of covenants: An empirical analysis of venture partnership agreements. *The Journal of Law and Economics, 39*(2), 463–498.

Grossman, H. I. (1994). Production, appropriation, and land reform. *The American Economic Review, 84*(3), 705–712.

Grover, V., Chiang, R. H., Liang, T. P., & Zhang, D. (2018). Creating strategic business value from big data analytics: A research framework. *Journal of Management Information Systems, 35*(2), 388–423.

Hadida, A. L., Lampel, J., Walls, W. D., & Joshi, A. (2021). Hollywood studio filmmaking in the age of Netflix: A tale of two institutional logics. *Journal of Cultural Economics, 45*, 213–238. https://doi.org/10.1007/s10824-020-09379-z

Harrison, A., Dalkiran, E., & Elsey, E. (2000). International business: global competition from a European perspective. *OUP Catalogue*.

Hawley, E. W. (2015). *The new deal and the problem of monopoly*. Princeton University Press.

Hayes, L. B. (2011). Global markets change Thai culture and create new dependencies. *Berkeley Center for Religion, Peace & World Affairs*. Retrieved from https://berkleycenter.georgetown.edu/posts/global-markets-change-thai-culture-and-create-new-dependencies

He, W., Wang, F. K., & Akula, V. (2017). Managing extracted knowledge from big social media data for business decision making. *Journal of Knowledge Management*.

Head, K., & Spencer, B. J. (2017). Oligopoly in international trade: Rise, fall and resurgence. *Canadian Journal of Economics/revue Canadienne D'économique, 50*(5), 1414–1444.

Huda, M., Qodriah, S. L., Rismayadi, B., Hananto, A., Kardiyati, E. N., Ruskam, A., & Nasir, B. M. (2019). Towards cooperative with competitive alliance: Insights into performance value in social entrepreneurship. In *Creating business value and competitive advantage with social entrepreneurship* (pp. 294–317).

Itani, O. S., Goad, E. A., & Jaramillo, F. (2019). Building customer relationships while achieving sales performance results: Is listening the holy grail of sales? *Journal of Business Research, 102*, 120–130.

Ivančić, V. (2013). The biggest failures in managing strategy implementation. *Interdisciplinary Management Research, 9*.

Ikechi, A., Chinenye, E. P., & Chiyem, O. (2017). Marketing mix concept: Blending the variables to suit the contemporary marketers. *International Academic Journal of Management and Marketing, 9*(1), 55–65.

Iyer, P., Davari, A., Zolfagharian, M., & Paswan, A. (2019). Market orientation, positioning strategy and brand performance. *Industrial Marketing Management, 81*, 16–29.

Jalkala, A. M., & Keränen, J. (2014). Brand positioning strategies for industrial firms providing customer solutions. *Journal of Business & Industrial Marketing*.

Jianyu, Z., Baizhou, L., Xi, X., Guangdong, W., & Tienan, W. (2018). Research on the characteristics of evolution in knowledge flow networks of strategic alliance under different resource allocation. *Expert Systems with Applications, 98*, 242–256.

Kale, P., Singh, H., & Perlmutter, H. (2000). Learning and protection of proprietary assets in strategic alliances: Building relational capital. *Strategic Management Journal, 21*(3), 217–237.

Kamariotou, M., & Kitsios, F. (2017). Information systems phases and firm performance: a conceptual framework. *Strategic Innovative Marketing*, 553–560.

Kaplan, R. S., & Norton, D. P. (2005). *Creating the office of strategy management*. Division of Research, Harvard Business School.

Katz, L. (2017). *Negotiating international business—Negotiating international business—The negotiator's reference guide to 50 countries around the world*. Booksurge.

Khalid, B., Chaveesuk, S., & Chaiyasoonthorn, W. (2021). MOOCS adoption in higher education: A management perspective. *Polish Journal of Management Studies, 23*(1), 239–256. https://doi.org/10.17512/pjms.2021.23.1.15

Khalid, B., Lis, M., Chaiyasoonthorn, W., & Cheevasuk, S. (2021). Factors influencing behavioral intention to use MOOCs. *Engineering Management in Production and Services, 13*(2), 83–95.

Kobayashi, J., Aritaka, N., Nozaki, I., Tabata, A., & Noda, S. (2021). COVID-19 control during a humanitarian crisis; the need for emergency response at the Thai-Myanmar border as an alternative channel. *Trop Med Health, 49*, 33. Retrieved from https://doi.org/10.1186/s41182-021-00323-1

Kotaskova, A., Belas, J., Bilan, Y., & Ajaz Khan, K. (2020). Significant aspects of managing personnel risk in the SME sector. *Management & Marketing. Challenges for the Knowledge Society, 15*(2), 203–218. https://doi.org/10.2478/mmcks-2020-0013

Levitt, T. (1983). Globalizations of markets. *Harvard Business Review, 61*(3), 69–81.

Lopatta, K., Jaeschke, R., Tchikov, M., & Lodhia, S. (2017). Corruption, corporate social responsibility and financial constraints: International firm-level evidence. *European Management Review, 14*(1), 47–65.

Lahtinen, V., Dietrich, T., & Rundle-Thiele, S. (2020). Long live the marketing mix. Testing the effectiveness of the commercial marketing mix in a social marketing context. *Journal of Social Marketing*.

Luo, Y. (2007). A coopetition perspective of global competition. *Journal of world business, 42*(2), 129–144.

Mahmutaj, L. R., Ramosaj, B., & Krasniqi, B.A. (2019). Exploring driving factors and challenges of innovation in service firms: Evidence from Kosovo. *International Journal of Technological Learning, Innovation and Development, 11*(3). https://doi.org/10.1504/IJTLID.2019.102675

McLean, S. (2010). *Business communication for success*. Flat World Knowledge.

Meekaewkunchorn, N., Szczepańska-Woszczyna, K., Muangmee, C., Kassakorn, N., & Khalid, B. (2021). Entrepreneurial orientation and SME performance: The mediating role of learning orientation. *Economics & Sociology, 14*(2), 294–312. https://doi.org/10.14254/2071-789X.2021/14-2/16

Merriman, K. K. (2017). *Valuation of human capital: Quantifying the importance of an assembled workforce*. Springer.

Mitchell, D. W., & Coles, C. B. (2004). Establishing a continuing business model innovation process. *Journal of business strategy*.

Morabito, V. (2017). *Business innovation through blockchain*. Cham: Springer International Publishing.

More than Just Smiles: Cultural Behaviors behind Key Market Trends in Thailand. (2018, June 11). *LABRAND*. Retrieved from https://www.labbrand.com/brandsource/more-than-just-smiles-cultural-behaviors-behind-key-market-trends-in-thailand

References

Muangmee, C., Kot, S., Meekaewkunchorn, N., Kassakorn, N., & Khalid, B. (2021). Factors determining the behavioral intention of using food delivery apps during COVID-19 pandemics. *Journal of Theoretical and Applied Electronic Commerce Research, 16*(5), 1297–1310. https://doi.org/10.3390/jtaer16050073

Muangmee, C., Dacko-Pikiewicz, Z., Meekaewkunchorn, N., Kassakorn, N., & Khalid, B. (2021). Green entrepreneurial orientation and green innovation in Small and Medium-Sized Enterprises (SMEs). *Social Sciences, 10*(4), 136. https://doi.org/10.3390/socsci10040136

Nguyen, N. T., & Tran, T. T. (2019). Raising opportunities in strategic alliance by evaluating efficiency of logistics companies in Vietnam: A case of Cat Lai Port. *Neural Computing and Applications, 31*(11), 7963–7974.

Ohmae, K. (1989). Managing in a borderless world. *Harvard Business Review, 67*(3), 152–161.

Olson, E. M., Slater, S. F., Hult, G. T. M., & Olson, K. M. (2018). The application of human resource management policies within the marketing organization: The impact on business and marketing strategy implementation. *Industrial Marketing Management, 69*, 62–73.

Parenti, M. U. (2017). Toward a theory of monopolistic competition. *Journal of Economic Theory, 167*, 86–115.

Pavlou, P. A., & El Sawy, O. A. (2006). From IT leveraging competence to competitive advantage in turbulent environments: The case of new product development. *Information Systems Research, 17*(3), 198–227.

Payutto, P. A. (2003). *The way of thinking according to Buddhist principles.* (9th ed.). Bangkok: Thammasat.

Perdomo-Ortiz, J., Gonzalez-Benito, J., & Galende, J. (2006). Total quality management as a forerunner of business innovation capability. *Technovation, 26*(10), 1170–1185.

Pearlson, K. E., Saunders, C. S., & Galletta, D. F. (2019). *Managing and using information systems: A strategic approach.* John Wiley & Sons.

Pi, S., Liu, S., & Liu, L. (2017). Dynamic competitive bevahior of enterprises in multi-network: Evidence from Chinese animation industry. *EURASIA Journal of Mathematics Science and Technology Education, 13*(8), 5185–5203. https://doi.org/10.12973/eurasia.2017.00993a

Place, K. (2019). Listening as the driver of public relations practice and communications strategy within a global public relations agency. *Public Relations Journal, 12*(3), 1–18.

Praveena, A., & Smys, S. (2017). Ensuring data security in cloud based social networks. In *2017 International Conference of Electronics, Communication and Aerospace Technology (ICECA)*, pp. 289–295.

Radosevic, S., & Yoruk, E. (2016). Why do we need a theory and metrics of technology upgrading? *Asian Journal of Technology Innovation, 24*(sup1), 8–32.

Rafique, W., & Jayaratne, S. (2020). Giving back to society: A recycling business venture. In *International Trade Forum*.

Ramalingam, B. & Prabhu, J. (2020). Innovation, development and COVID-19: Challenges, opportunities and ways forward. *Organisation for Economic Co-operation and Development.* Retrieved from https://www.oecd.org/coronavirus/policy-responses/innovation-development-and-covid-19-challenges-opportunities-and-ways-forward-0c976158/

Ramsing, L. (2009). Project communication in a strategic internal perspective. *Corporate Communications: An International Journal.*

Reed, K., Goolsby, J. R., & Johnston, M. K. (2016). Listening in and out: Listening to customers and employees to strengthen an integrated market-oriented system. *Journal of Business Research, 69*(9), 3591–3599.

Ries, A., & Trout, J. (1981). *Positioning: The battle for the mind.*

Sahut, J. M., & Peris-Ortiz, M. (2014). Small business, innovation, and entrepreneurship. *Small Business Economics, 42*(4), 663–668.

Sarmaniotis, C., Wickens, E., Singh, J., Kalafatis, S. P., & Ledden, L. (2014). Consumer perceptions of cobrands: The role of brand positioning strategies. *Marketing Intelligence & Planning.*

Sawmong, S. (2020). A study of rice mill innovation for using in household that effects the marketing mix satisfaction of farmers in Thailand. *Journal of Public Affairs.* https://doi.org/10.1002/pa.2315

Sawmong, S. (2020). Influence of organizational factors on workers' desires: An investigation of manufacturing industry. *Polish Journal of Management Studies, 22*(2), 518–534.

Schiemann, W. A., Seibert, J. H., & Blankenship, M. H. (2018). Putting human capital analytics to work: Predicting and driving business success. *Human Resource Management, 57*(3), 795–807.

Servaes, J. (1990). Technology transfer in thailand: For whom and for what? *Telematics and Informatics, 7*(1), 9–25.

Setti, I., Sommovigo, V., & Argentero, P. (2020). Enhancing expatriates' assignments success: the relationships between cultural intelligence, cross-cultural adaptation and performance. *Current Psychology*, 1–21.

Slater, S. F., & Olson, E. M. (2001). Marketing's contribution to the implementation of business strategy: An empirical analysis. *Strategic Management Journal, 22*(11), 1055-1067.

Sprinkle, G. B., & Maines, L. A. (2010). The benefits and costs of corporate social responsibility. *Business Horizons, 53*(5), 445–453.

Sripaipan, C. (1991). Technology upgrading in Thailand: A strategic perspective. *Quarterly Review, 6*(4), 3–10.

Suganthi, L. (2020). Investigating the relationship between corporate social responsibility and market, cost and environmental performance for sustainable business. *South African Journal of Business Management, 51*(1), 13.

Tosti, D. T. (2007). Aligning the culture and strategy for success. *Performance Improvement, 46*(1), 21–25.

Taylor, C. (2014). Consumer privacy in oligopolistic markets: Winners, losers, and welfare. *International Journal of Industrial Organization, 34*, 80–84.

Tallman, S., Luo, Y., & Buckley, P. J. (2018). Business models in global competition. *Global Strategy Journal, 8*(4), 517–535.

Thomas, D. C. (2006). Domain and development of cultural intelligence: The importance of mindfulness. *Group & Organization Management, 31*(1), 78–99.

Thomas, D. C., & Inkson, K. (2005). Cultural intelligence: People skills for a global workplace. *Consulting to Management, 16*(1), 5–9.

Thomas, D. C., & Inkson, K. (2004). *Cultural intelligence: People skills for global business*. Berrett-Koehler.

Verčič, A. T., & Ćorić, D. S. (2018). The relationship between reputation, employer branding and corporate social responsibility. *Public Relations Review, 44*(4), 444–452.

Van Mierlo, J., Bondarouk, T., & Sanders, K. (2018). The dynamic nature of HRM implementation: A structuration perspective. *The International Journal of Human Resource Management, 29*(22), 3026–3045.

Venkitachalam, K., & Ambrosini, V. (2017). A triadic link between knowledge management, information technology and business strategies. *Knowledge Management Research & Practice, 15*(2), 192–200.

Vallée, B. (2001). Dynamical sources in information theory: Fundamental intervals and word prefixes. *Algorithmica, 29*(1), 262–306.

Wall, W. P. (2021). Determinants of SMEs' performance—from business strategy to innovation. *Polish Journal of Management Studies, 23*(2), 537–554.

Wall, W. P. (2021). The comparison of the TQM practices and quality performance between manufacturing & service sectors. *Polish Journal of Management Studies, 23*(1), 436–452.

Wall, W.P., Chaiwattanaporn, S., Pongwiritthon, R., & Nithisathian, K. (2020). The role and impact of business process management of Thai construction industry toward AEC and ASEAN. *Journal of Suvarnabhumi Institute of Technology, 6*(2). Retrieved from https://so04.tci-thaijo.org/index.php/svittj/article/view/181627

Weger, H., Jr., Castle Bell, G., Minei, E. M., & Robinson, M. C. (2014). The relative effectiveness of active listening in initial interactions. *International Journal of Listening, 28*(1), 13–31.

Xing Li, J. (2015). Factor distortion and total factor productivity——The empirical analysis based on monopoly competition model. *Nanjing Business Review, 1*, 3.

References

Yan, M. R. (2017). Strategic product innovations and dynamic pricing models in oligopolistic market.

YvKoff, L. (2020, September 10). To compete with uber and lyft, taxis make the switch to upfront pricing. *Forbes*. Retrieved from https://www.forbes.com/sites/lianeyvkoff/2020/09/10/to-compete-with-uber-and-lyft-taxis-make-the-switch-to-upfront-pricing/?sh=24ccdcdc6b70

Zeuthen, F. (2018). *Problems of monopoly and economic warfare* (Vol. 25). Routledge.

Zwikael, O. C. (2018). Project benefit management: Setting effective target benefits. *International Journal of Project Management, 36*(4), 650–658.

Printed in the United States
by Baker & Taylor Publisher Services